Realistic Ray Tracing
Second Edition

Realistic Ray Tracing
Second Edition

Peter Shirley
R. Keith Morley

A K Peters
Natick, Massachusetts

Editorial, Sales, and Customer Service Office

A K Peters, Ltd.
5 Commonwealth Road, Suite 2C
Natick, MA 01760
www.akpeters.com

Originally printed in hardcover.
First paperback printing, 2009
    ISBN 978-1-56881-461-2

Library of Congress Cataloging-in-Publication Data

Shirley, P. (Peter), 1963–.
  Realistic ray tracing / Peter Shirley, R. Keith Morley.–2nd ed.
      p. cm.
    ISBN 1-56881-198-5
    1. Computer graphics. I. Morley, R. Keith. 1976- II. Title.

T385.S438 2003   2003051411
006.6′2--dc21

Printed in the United States of America
13 12 11 10   10 9 8 7 6 5 4 3

Contents

Preface

The main code the authors use to generate images is a *ray tracer*. The basic ray tracing concepts were developed and popularized primarily by Turner Whitted in the late 1970s and early 1980s. These were expanded into *probabilistic ray tracing* by Rob Cook and Jim Kajiya in the mid 1980s. Most of the book's content is due to these pioneers. Of course, many other people dealt with tracking the movement of rays around an environment, such as Appel and Kay, and with luck, a full history of computer graphics will get written up someday.

The content of this book grew from several classes and seminars at Indiana University, Cornell University, and the University of Utah. The notes from these classes have grown into this book. This book is not meant to be a survey, and we hope that it doesn't read like one. If you want to learn *everything* about ray tracing, there is a variety of books that you should read, but the most complete collection is the online *Ray Tracing News*, edited by Eric Haines. This is a remarkably complete discussion of ray tracing issues by hard-core ray tracing geeks.

This is the second edition of this book and the changes have been substantial. Most significantly, we have added C++ code rather than relying on pseudocode. All of this code is available at our web site. In addition to revising the material from the first edition, we have added chapters on photon mapping and participating media. We have also replaced the chapter on uniform grids with a new chapter on bounding volume hierarchies because we think these are both easier to implement and superior in overall performance. The discussion of reflection models is completely new. We believe the new discussion is simpler and provides a more straightforward implementation.

ABOUT THE COVER

The cover image was modeled by the second author using the *Maya* modeling package, generously donated to our research group by Alias—Wavefront. It was rendered using our *Galileo* renderer, whose guts are described this book.

The image was rendered at a 600 x 800 resolution using 1600 samples per pixel. On 64 600Mhz processors the image took about 10 minutes to render.

ACKNOWLEDGEMENTS

This book would not have been possible without the many students who have helped determine which presentation methods work best. In addition, much of the material in the book has been taught to us by our teachers, students, and co-workers. In particular, Jim Arvo, Teresa Hughey, Steve Marschner, Don Mitchell, Steve Parker, Greg Rogers, Brian Smits, and Kelvin Sung helped the first author with the basics of programming and ray tracing. The buddha model which appears in images throughout the book is from Stanford Graphics Laboratory's scanning repository (http://graphics.stanford.edu/data/3Dscanrep/).

Michael Herf, Steve Marschner, Nelson Max, Peter-Pike Sloan, and Mike Stark were extremely helpful in improving the book. Many people found errors in or made suggestions for improvements to the first edition if the book and for this we thank them: Patrick Angel, Steve Barrus, Bobby Bodenheimer, Dean Brederson, Brian Budge, Phil Dutre, Alexander Keller, Gordon Kindlmann, Eric Haines, Randall Hopper, Henrik Wann Jensen, Ray Jones, William Martin, Tomas Moller, Nelson Max, Niels Holm Olsen, Matt Ownby, Erik Reinhard, and Jason Smith.

The first author's parents, Bob Shirley and Molly Lind, provided some crucial babysitting that allowed the first edition of this book to get done, and his wife Jean did all the work in our household for a year, without which the book never would have happened.

The second author's wife, Jamie Morley, showed infinite patience in dealing with a husband who thinks he can be a fulltime student, fulltime researcher, and an author all at the same time. His parents never lost faith in their son.

Alice and Klaus Peters deserve special credit for encouraging us to write this book, and we are very grateful to the publisher of this book, A K Peters, for their great dedication to quality publications. The A K Peters editors for this book, Heather Holcombe and Sarah Gillis, were a pleasure to work with and improved the manuscripts greatly.

Peter Shirley
R. Keith Morley
Salt Lake City, USA
April, 2003

Introduction

This book will show you how to implement a *ray tracer*. A ray tracer uses simple algorithms to make realistic pictures. Ray tracing is becoming more and more popular because of increases in computing power and because of its ability to cleanly deal with effects such as shadows and transparency. It has been used in feature animations, and it is just a matter of time before it is used to drive a video game. Most importantly, writing ray tracing code is fun, and it is a great way to learn many graphics concepts.

An overview of a ray tracing program is shown in Figure 1. Here, the eye is at point **e** and it is looking through a 3D "window" at two shaded spheres. For each point on the window, we send a 3D "ray" to that point and extend it into the scene as shown by the arrow and dotted line. Whatever this ray hits first is what is seen in that pixel. Each pixel can be computed independently by simple computations to form the image shown in the lower left of the figure. The two main tasks of the program are determining what point on what object is hit, and what color that point is. The first task will require intersecting 3D lines with surfaces such as spheres, which will require some mathematics. Determining the color will require some simple physics and the generation of rays from the intersection point to see how the world "looks" to that point. All of this will turn out to be elegant, and will thus yield a clean and maintainable program.

The book is divided into short chapters, each of which introduces one new feature or concept for your ray tracer. Our general philosophy is that clean mathematics maps directly to clean code. The text will be very detail-oriented. Little will be left as an exercise to the reader. We use the vocabulary of an object-oriented language such as C++ or Java, but the principles apply to any language. We have chosen to give our sample code in C++. This is because C++ has the object-oriented capabilities that allow for a clean structure, as well as the ability to handle fairly low-level optimizations. In addition, the operator-overloading of C++ makes the high-level routines easier to read than they would be in languages that lack that feature.

There are two basic types of math that are covered in the book. The first is basic vector geometry. This is used for managing decisions such as what object

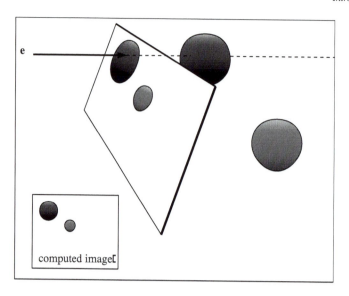

Figure 1. An overview of the ray tracing concept.

is seen in a given direction. The second is *Monte Carlo integration*. This is used to compute various averages such as the average pixel color. Such averaging is accomplished using statistics in an analogous way that opinion polls are used to gauge public sentiment. We will defer the details of Monte Carlo integration until after we cover the details of writing the geometric engine, and thus we do some "hand waving" about random sampling early on so we can concentrate on geometry at first. Concerned readers should be relieved that we will cover all of the details by the end of the book.

We assume some comfort with high school mathematics in general. If you are math-phobic, now is the time to cure yourself; take it slowly, and keep the algebra firmly mapped to the geometry. Read every section carefully, and go on to the next section only when you are ready. Just don't give up! A firm grasp of the fundamentals is hard to get, but will last a lifetime.

We build up the ray tracer one step at a time, and your program will expand with each chapter. There will be images in each chapter you should duplicate. We emphasize a clean program and leave efficiency as a second priority. Clean programs are usually fast programs, so this won't cause as many problems as you might expect. Our own code is given at the end of each chapter, and it is downloadable at http://www.cs.utah.edu/~shirley/galileo/. At the end, you will have a compact and powerful program. This program can be improved in the many ways discussed in the last chapter, but it will be very useful as is. Let's begin!

NOTES

Throughout the book, we assume that light obeys the rules of geometric optics and that polarization does not exist. This is of course not true; there are many examples where polarization is very important, as shown in *Polarized Light in Nature* (Konnen, Cambridge University Press, 1965). The same is true for diffraction, which is responsible for the vibrant colors of many animals' exteriors. However, for at least the next couple of decades, a lack of polarization or physical optics effects will not be the biggest limitation of rendering codes. Fluorescence is an important effect, especially in man-made environments where almost every bright color is partially due to fluorescence. The details of adding polarization and fluorescence to a ray tracer can be found in "Combined Rendering of Polarization and Fluorescence Effects" (Wilke, Tobler, and Purgathofer, *E*urographics Workshop on Rendering, 2001). We do not talk about *radiosity*, which already has three good books devoted to it: *Radiosity and Realistic Image Synthesis* (Cohen and Wallace, Morgan Kaufmann, 1993), *Radiosity and Global Illumination* (Sillion and Puesch, Morgan Kaufmann, 1994), and *Radiosity: A Programmer's Perspective*, (Ashdown, John Wiley & Sons, 1994). There are also many topics related to Monte Carlo sampling, variants of path tracing, and hybrid algorithms which will be skipped entirely. For a broader treatment of image synthesis algorithms, the reader should consult *Principles of Digital Image Synthesis* (Glassner, Morgan Kaufmann, 1995) and *Realistic Image Synthesis Using Photon Mapping* (Jensen, A K Peters, 2001). For an excellent treatment of interactive rendering, see *Real-Time Rendering, 2nd Ed.* (Möller and Haines, A K Peters, 2002). Readers who need a general refresher on the type of math used in graphics will enjoy *3D Math Primer for Graphics and Game Development* (Dunn and Parberry, Wordware Publishing, 2002).

1 | Getting Started

Underlying any graphics program is utility code that allows us to think and program at a higher level. In ray tracing programs, there are certain pieces of utility code that pop up repeatedly and are worth coding up front. This chapter describes that code.

1.1 CODE OPTIMIZATION

Spending a little time on code optimization during development will pay off greatly in the long run. Starting with clean math and developing clean code is the first step. A good compiler will do most of the rest for you. However, there are several techniques that will help shorten your render times.

All of the code in this book can be written using floats without concern for loss of needed accuracy. Switching from double precision to single precision will decrease your render times on most architectures because of better cache utilization and possibly faster arithmetic operations. If you anticipate needing high precision, you should use a typedef statement to allow a compile time switch between single and double precision.

For maximum efficiency it is crucial to use aggressive inlining on short functions that are called frequently. Inline functions should be used instead of C Pre-Processor (CPP) macros when possible since they are safer and usually just as fast. However, it is also important not to overuse inlining, particularly for large functions. Such overuse not only leads to difficult debugging, but it can cause assembly level code bloat that actually slows run times.

Once you have a working ray tracer, you can take additional steps to speed things up. The acceleration data structures discussed later in the book give you, by far, the most bang for your buck. A good strategy would be to implement an acceleration structure and then use profiling tools to target the problem areas of your program. One important use of profilers is to ensure that functions are getting inlined as you intended. Simply run a profiler in function cost mode and inlined functions shouldn't show up at all on the profile since the function call is being replaced with the actual function body. Once all small functions are being inlined properly, you can focus on optimizing the high cost functions.

1.2   RGB COLORS

Your output image will be in a "red-green-blue" color space, referred to for the rest of the book as *RGB*. You should have three real numbers to represent the three components.

You will want to make all the "normal" arithmetic operations work with RGBs. Given RGBs a, b, and scalar k, the following operators should be implemented:

$$
\begin{aligned}
+\mathbf{a} &= \left(a_r, a_g, a_b\right), \\
-\mathbf{a} &= \left(-a_r, -a_g, -a_b\right), \\
k * \mathbf{a} &= \left(ka_r, ka_g, ka_b\right), \\
\mathbf{a} * k &= \left(ka_r, ka_g, ka_b\right), \\
\mathbf{a}/k &= \left(a_r/k, a_g/k, a_b/k\right), \\
\mathbf{a} + \mathbf{b} &= \left(a_r + b_r, a_g + b_g, a_b + b_b\right), \\
\mathbf{a} - \mathbf{b} &= \left(a_r - b_r, a_g - b_g, a_b - b_b\right), \\
\mathbf{a} * \mathbf{b} &= \left(a_r b_r, a_g b_g, a_b b_b\right), \\
\mathbf{a}/\mathbf{b} &= \left(a_r/b_r, a_g/b_g, a_b/b_b\right), \\
\mathbf{a} + = \mathbf{b} &= \left(\mathbf{a} \leftarrow \mathbf{a} + \mathbf{b}\right), \\
\mathbf{a} - = \mathbf{b} &= \left(\mathbf{a} \leftarrow \mathbf{a} - \mathbf{b}\right), \\
\mathbf{a} * = \mathbf{b} &= \left(\mathbf{a} \leftarrow \mathbf{a} * \mathbf{b}\right), \\
\mathbf{a}/ = \mathbf{b} &= \left(\mathbf{a} \leftarrow \mathbf{a}/\mathbf{b}\right).
\end{aligned}
$$

1.3   IMAGES

You will want to use simple 2D arrays of RGB colors both for storing your computed image and for storing texture maps.

You will want to write a few utility functions to output images, either as they are computed or as they are finished. If you output to a file, use whatever format is easiest to implement. You can always convert the files you want to save to a compact or portable format offline. A few software packages that can convert image formats and perform other image manipulations are discussed in the notes section at the end of this chapter.

For now, assume the convention that colors whose components are all zero are black, and colors whose components are all one are white. That is, $RGB = (1, 1, 1)$ represents the color white. You must usually convert each of these numbers $f \in [0, 1)$ into a one byte quantity $i \in \{0, 1, \ldots, 255\}$, where $[0, 1)$ indicates the interval of numbers between zero to one including zero but not one. This is accomplished with $i = int(256 * f)$. If you are not sure that f is in that range, an "if" should be added to force i within the range. On most systems, the intensity on the screen is nonlinear; $i = 128$ is significantly less than half as bright as $i = 255$. The standard way to handle this is to assume the screen or printer has a "power curve" described by a parameter gamma γ,

$$\text{luminance} \propto \left(\frac{i}{255} \right)^{\gamma}.$$

Thus the "gamma-corrected" image that you output should be

$$i = int(256 * f^{\frac{1}{\gamma}}).$$

This formula assumes f is less than one, because $f = 1$ would yield $i = 256$, which would be an overflow. However, in practice, $f > 1$ can occur in programs, so clamping is needed in any case. The values of gamma for most systems range from 1.7 to 2.3. Most Linux boxes and PCs are 2.2 and most Macs are 1.8. The emerging standard "sRGB" uses gamma 2.2. See www.srgb.com for details.

1.4 VECTORS

A *vector* describes an n-dimensional offset or location. For our purposes, we need 2D and 3D vectors. Rather than trying to write an n-dimensional class, you should write two classes *vector2* and *vector3* to maximize efficiency.

For the actual storage of the (x, y, z) coordinates you should use an array. For example, you should have *data[3]* rather than x, y, z. This allows a member function *element(i)* which returns the ith data element without using any *if* statements. For example, *v.element(1)* should return the y coordinate of v. This is most efficient if an array is used.

You may want to make a separate point class to store locations, but our current belief is that although this improves type checking and aids implicit documentation, it makes coding more awkward in practice. We advocate just using vectors to store points; the value of the vector is the displacement from the origin the point.

The *length* of a vector $\mathbf{a} = (a_x, a_y, a_z)$ is given by

$$\|\mathbf{a}\| = \sqrt{a_x^2 + a_y^2 + a_z^2}.$$

You should have member functions that return $\|\mathbf{a}\|$ and $\|\mathbf{a}\|^2$. If the length of $\mathbf{v}$ is one, it is called a *unit vector*. You may want a special class for that, and you may not. It strengthens type checking, but can interfere with efficiency and increases the number of possibly nonobvious type conversions.

You will want to make all the "normal" arithmetic operations for vectors. Given vectors $\mathbf{a}$, $\mathbf{b}$, and scalar k, the following operators should be implemented:

$$
\begin{aligned}
+\mathbf{a} &= (a_x, a_y, a_z), \\
-\mathbf{a} &= (-a_x, -a_y, -a_z), \\
k \star \mathbf{a} &= (ka_x, ka_y, ka_z), \\
\mathbf{a} \star k &= (ka_x, ka_y, ka_z), \\
\mathbf{a}/k &= (a_x/k, a_y/k, a_z/k), \\
\mathbf{a} + \mathbf{b} &= (a_x + b_x, a_y + b_y, a_z + b_z), \\
\mathbf{a} - \mathbf{b} &= (a_x - b_x, a_y - b_y, a_z - b_z), \\
\mathbf{a}\star = k &= (\mathbf{a} \leftarrow \mathbf{a} \star k), \\
\mathbf{a}/ = k &= (\mathbf{a} \leftarrow \mathbf{a}/k), \\
\mathbf{a}+ = \mathbf{b} &= (\mathbf{a} \leftarrow \mathbf{a} + \mathbf{b}), \\
\mathbf{a}- = \mathbf{b} &= (\mathbf{a} \leftarrow \mathbf{a} - \mathbf{b}).
\end{aligned}
$$

There are two important operators for 3D vectors: the *dot product* ($\cdot$) and the *cross product* ($\times$). To compute these, use the following formulae:

$$
\begin{aligned}
\mathbf{a} \cdot \mathbf{b} &= a_x b_x + a_y b_y + a_z b_z, \\
\mathbf{a} \times \mathbf{b} &= (\ a_y b_z - a_z b_y,\ a_z b_x - a_x b_z,\ a_x b_y - a_y b_x\ ).
\end{aligned}
$$

Note that the dot product returns a scalar and the cross product returns a 3D vector. The dot product has a property that is used in an amazing number of ways in various graphics programs:

$$\mathbf{a} \cdot \mathbf{b} = \|\mathbf{a}\| \, \|\mathbf{b}\| \, \cos\theta,$$

where θ is the angle between $\mathbf{a}$ and $\mathbf{b}$. The most common use of the dot product is to compute the cosine of the angle between two vectors. If $\mathbf{a}$ and $\mathbf{b}$ are unit vectors, this is accomplished with three multiplications and two additions.

The cross product $\mathbf{a} \times \mathbf{b}$ has a different, but equally interesting, geometric property. First, the length of the resulting vector is related to $\sin\theta$:

$$\|\mathbf{a} \times \mathbf{b}\| = \|\mathbf{a}\|\|\mathbf{b}\| \sin\theta.$$

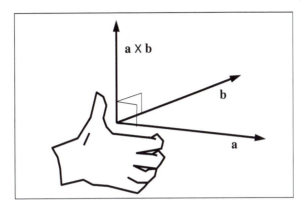

Figure 1.1. To establish whether $\mathbf{a} \times \mathbf{b}$ points "up" or "down," place your right hand in such a way that your wrist is at the bases of $\mathbf{a}$ and $\mathbf{b}$, and your palm will push the arrow of $\mathbf{a}$ toward the arrow of $\mathbf{b}$. You thumb will point in the direction of the resulting cross product. Since $\mathbf{x}$, $\mathbf{y}$, and $\mathbf{z}$ obey this, they are referred to as a "right-handed" coordinate system.

In addition, $\mathbf{a} \times \mathbf{b}$ is perpendicular to both $\mathbf{a}$ and $\mathbf{b}$. Note that there are only two possible directions for such a vector. For example, if the vectors in the direction of the x-, y-, and z-axes are given by

$$
\begin{aligned}
\mathbf{x} &= (1,0,0), \\
\mathbf{y} &= (0,1,0), \\
\mathbf{z} &= (0,0,1),
\end{aligned}
$$

then $\mathbf{x} \times \mathbf{y}$ must be in the plus or minus $\mathbf{z}$ direction. You can compute this to determine that, in fact, $\mathbf{x} \times \mathbf{y} = \mathbf{z}$. But how do we visualize what the geometric configuration of these vectors is? To settle this, a convention is used: the *right-hand rule*. This rule in illustrated in Figure 1.1. Note that this implies the useful properties:

$$
\begin{aligned}
\mathbf{x} \times \mathbf{y} &= +\mathbf{z}, \\
\mathbf{y} \times \mathbf{x} &= -\mathbf{z}, \\
\mathbf{y} \times \mathbf{z} &= +\mathbf{x}, \\
\mathbf{z} \times \mathbf{y} &= -\mathbf{x}, \\
\mathbf{z} \times \mathbf{x} &= +\mathbf{y}, \\
\mathbf{x} \times \mathbf{z} &= -\mathbf{y}.
\end{aligned}
$$

1.5 ORTHONORMAL BASES AND FRAMES

Graphics programs usually manage many coordinate systems. For example, in a flight simulator, the airplane is stored in the coordinate system aligned with the fuselage, wings, and tail. The orientation part of such a coordinate system is stored as three *orthonormal* vectors $\mathbf{u}$, $\mathbf{v}$, and $\mathbf{w}$, which are unit length, mutually perpendicular, and right-handed ($\mathbf{u} \times \mathbf{v} = \mathbf{w}$). These three vectors are called the *basis vectors* of the coordinate system. As a set, they are an *orthonormal basis* (ONB).

The $\mathbf{x}$, $\mathbf{y}$, and $\mathbf{z}$ vectors form a special ONB called the *canonical basis*. This is the natural basis of our program, and all other bases are stored in terms of it. For example, any vector can be stored in xyz coordinates:

$$\mathbf{a} = (a_x, a_y, a_z) = a_x\mathbf{x} + a_y\mathbf{y} + a_z\mathbf{z}.$$

We are so familiar with this that we sometimes forget what these coordinates mean. The coordinates (a_x, a_y, a_z) are computed by dot the product as

$$
\begin{aligned}
a_x &= \mathbf{a} \cdot \mathbf{x}, \\
a_y &= \mathbf{a} \cdot \mathbf{y}, \\
a_z &= \mathbf{a} \cdot \mathbf{z}.
\end{aligned}
$$

The same would apply for any ONB. For example,

$$\mathbf{a} = (\mathbf{a} \cdot \mathbf{u})\mathbf{u} + (\mathbf{a} \cdot \mathbf{v})\mathbf{v} + (\mathbf{a} \cdot \mathbf{w})\mathbf{w}.$$

In programs we would often store these coordinates as (a_u, a_v, a_w). You might have two different vectors declared *a* and *a-uvw* that have different numbers in them, but represent the same directions. Note that we do not say the first vector is *a-xyz*—the default coordinate system is the canonical one. These vectors are the same geometrically even though they have different components. You would multiply them by different basis vectors before you would compare their coordinates. As you will see, we will use a noncanonical coordinate system when it is convenient, and that will make *a-xyz* have elements like $(7, 0, 0)$ or some other simple set of numbers because we are in a "natural" coordinate system. This may all sound like a pain, but stick with it because your program will be simpler and more efficient.

You should add some constructors or utility functions for ONBs. For example, you should make one *construct-from-uv* that takes two vectors a and b and produces an ONB where $\mathbf{u}$ is parallel to a, $\mathbf{v}$ is in the plane of a and b, and $\mathbf{w}$ is parallel to a × b. To accomplish this, proceed with the following assignments:

$$\mathbf{u} = \frac{\mathbf{a}}{\|\mathbf{a}\|},$$

$$\mathbf{w} = \frac{\mathbf{a} \times \mathbf{b}}{\|\mathbf{a} \times \mathbf{b}\|},$$

$$\mathbf{v} = \mathbf{w} \times \mathbf{u}.$$

Note that neither a nor b need be unit length, but neither can be zero length, and they cannot be parallel. Also note that the order of these operations must be as above. You should make five other constructors. The first is *construct-from-vu* which makes v parallel to the first vector. The other four are for *vw*, *wv*, *uw*, and *wu*.

Sometimes you want a coordinate system where one of the vectors has a particular direction, and the other two basis vectors can be arbitrary as long as they make a valid ONB. So implement a function *construct-from-w* which makes w parallel to a. Unfortunately, this requires an *if*:

$$\mathbf{m} = (0,1,0)$$

$$\mathbf{n} = (1,0,0)$$

$$\mathbf{w} = \frac{\mathbf{a}}{\|\mathbf{a}\|}$$

$$\mathbf{u} = \mathbf{w} \times \mathbf{m}$$

$$\text{if } \|\mathbf{u}\|^2 < \epsilon \text{ then}$$

$$\mathbf{u} = \mathbf{w} \times \mathbf{n}$$

$$\mathbf{v} = \mathbf{w} \times \mathbf{u}.$$

Once you have an ONB defined by u, v, and w, it is very easy to convert from $\mathbf{a} = (a_x, a_y, a_z)$ back and forth to $\mathbf{a}_{uvw} = (a_u, a_v, a_w)$:

$$a_u = \mathbf{a} \cdot \mathbf{u},$$

$$a_v = \mathbf{a} \cdot \mathbf{v},$$

$$a_w = \mathbf{a} \cdot \mathbf{w},$$

$$\mathbf{a} = a_u \mathbf{u} + a_v \mathbf{v} + a_w \mathbf{w}.$$

Note that the asymmetry of these equations arises because a has components stored in the canonical coordinate system while $\mathbf{a}_{uvw}$ does not.

To define a whole coordinate system, you will also need an origin point. This origin combined with an orthonormal basis can be called a *frame of reference* or *frame*. Define a class frame which is just an ONB and a point. It needs no member functions other than for access and construction.

1.6   DYNAMIC LENGTH ARRAYS

When writing a ray tracer you will often find the need for a list data structure that can grow to an arbitrary size. You might automatically think of the C++ Standard Template Library to fill this need. However, the STL's linked list classes do not work well for our purposes due to their slow access time. Therefore we recommend you write a simple array class that uses a C-style array as its base representation. The class will be easy to write due to a few constraints we can impose: data can only be added to the end of the list and data does not need to be removed.

1.7   RANDOM NUMBER GENERATOR

We recommend using a your own random number generator in your raytracer. While the cstdlib's *drand48()* is fairly fast and has good distribution properties, it is not portable and cannot be used if you decide to parallelize your raytracer in the future.

1.8   C++ CODE

You will find that we do not strictly adhere to conventional object-oriented dogma. We tend to use C++ as a better C. One thing to note is the fact that we do not use data protection within our classes. This is due to the fact that for some compilers, direct access to the data members is faster than using a function to access the data. We use data access functions in most of our code but drop down to direct access in critical sections.

1.8.1   RGB Class

One important decision when writing an RGB class is where to clamp your RGB values. A simple check within your constructor and assignment operators will ensure that you never have out of range values. We have left clamping up to the user of the class in order to avoid the significant performance hit associated with embedded clamping.

```
// rgb.h

#ifndef _RGB_H_
#define _RGB_H_ 1

#include <iostream.h>

class rgb
```

```
{
public:
  rgb() { _r = _g = _b = 0; }
  rgb(float red, float green, float blue);
  rgb(const rgb & original) { *this = original; }

  void setRed(float red)     { _r = red; }
  void setGreen(float green) { _g = green; }
  void setBlue(float blue)   { _b = blue; }

  // these operators perform no clamping
  rgb& operator=(const rgb & right_op);
  rgb& operator+=(const rgb & right_op);
  rgb& operator*=(const rgb & right_op);
  rgb& operator/=(const rgb & right_op);
  rgb& operator*=(float right_op);
  rgb& operator/=(float right_op);

  rgb operator+()const { return *this; }
  rgb operator-()const { return rgb(-_r, -_g, -_b); }

  float r() const { return _r; }
  float g() const { return _g; }
  float b() const { return _b; }

  void clamp();

  friend ostream& operator<<(ostream & out, const rgb & the_rgb);
  friend rgb operator*(const rgb& c, float f);
  friend rgb operator*(float f, const rgb& c);
  friend rgb operator/(const rgb& c, float f);
  friend rgb operator*(const rgb& c1, const rgb& c2);
  friend rgb operator/(const rgb& c1, const rgb& c2);
  friend rgb operator+(const rgb& c1, const rgb& c2);

  float _r;
  float _g;
  float _b;
};

inline rgb::rgb(float red, float green, float blue)
: _r(red), _g(green), _b(blue) {}

inline rgb& rgb::operator+=(const rgb & right_op) {
    *this = *this + right_op;
```

```
    return *this;
}

inline rgb& rgb::operator*=(float right_op) {
    *this = *this * right_op;
    return *this;
}

inline rgb& rgb::operator/=(float right_op) {
    *this = *this / right_op;
    return *this;
}

inline rgb& rgb::operator*=(const rgb & right_op) {
    *this = *this * right_op;
    return *this;
}

inline rgb& rgb::operator/=(const rgb & right_op) {
    *this = *this / right_op;
    return *this;
}

inline rgb& rgb::operator=(const rgb & right_op) {
  _r = right_op._r;
  _g = right_op._g;
  _b = right_op._b;
  return *this;
}

inline void rgb::clamp() {
    if (_r > 1.0f) _r = 1.0f;
    if (_g > 1.0f) _g = 1.0f;
    if (_b > 1.0f) _b = 1.0f;
    if (_r < 0.0f) _r = 0.0f;
    if (_g < 0.0f) _g = 0.0f;
    if (_b < 0.0f) _b = 0.0f;
}

inline ostream& operator<<(ostream & out, const rgb & the_rgb) {
  out << the_rgb._r << ' '
      << the_rgb._g << ' '
      << the_rgb._b << ' ';
  return out;
}
```

```
inline rgb operator*(const rgb& c, float f)
{ return rgb(c._r*f, c._g*f, c._b*f); }

inline rgb operator*(float f, const rgb& c)
{ return rgb(c._r*f, c._g*f, c._b*f); }

inline rgb operator/(const rgb& c, float f)
{ return rgb(c._r/f, c._g/f, c._b/f); }

inline rgb operator*(const rgb& c1, const rgb& c2)
{ return rgb(c1._r*c2._r, c1._g*c2._g, c1._b*c2._b); }

inline rgb operator/(const rgb& c1, const rgb& c2)
{ return rgb(c1._r/c2._r, c1._g/c2.g(), c1._b/c2._b); }

inline rgb operator+(const rgb& c1, const rgb& c2)
{ return rgb(c1._r+c2._r, c1._g+c2._g, c1._b+c2._b); }

#endif // _RGB_H_
```

1.8.2 Image Class

This simple image class implements functions to read and write binary Portable PixMaps (PPMs). Image manipulation utilities such as xv or gimp can be used to change PPMs to any other standard file format.

```
// Image.h

#ifndef _IMAGE_H_
#define _IMAGE_H_ 1

#include <cmath>
#include <string>
#include <fstream>
#include "rgb.h"
using namespace std;

class Image
{
public:
  Image();
  // initializes raster to default rgb color
  Image(int width, int height );
  // initializes raster to 'background'
  Image(int width, int height, rgb background);
  // returns false if x or y are out of bounds, else true
```

```
  bool set(int x, int y, const rgb & color);
  void gammaCorrect(float gamma);
  // outputs PPM image to 'out'
  void writePPM(ostream& out);
  void readPPM (string file_name);

private:
  rgb** raster;
  int nx;  // raster width
  int ny;  // raster height
};

#endif // _IMAGE_H_



// Image.cc

#include "Image.h"
#include <iostream>
using namespace std;

Image::Image()
{}

Image::Image(int width, int height)
{
  nx = width;
  ny = height;

  // allocate memory for raster
  raster = new rgb*[nx];
  for (int i = 0; i < nx; i++)
    raster[i] = new rgb[ny];
}

Image::Image(int width, int height, rgb background)
{
  nx = width;
  ny = height;

  // allocate memory for raster
  raster = new rgb*[nx];
  for (int i = 0; i < nx; i++)
  {
    raster[i] = new rgb[ny];
```

```cpp
      // assign 'background' to each element
      for (int j = 0; j < ny; j++)
        raster[i][j] = background;
  }
}

bool Image::set(int x, int y, const rgb& color)
{
   // check for out of bounds error
   if (0 > x || x > nx) return false;
   if (0 > y || y > ny) return false;

   raster[x][y] = color;
}

void Image::gammaCorrect(float gamma)
{
   rgb temp;
   float power = 1.0 / gamma;
   for (int i = 0; i < nx; i++)
      for (int j = 0; j < ny; j++)
      {
 temp = raster[i][j];
 raster[i][j] = rgb(pow(temp.r(), power),
                    pow(temp.g(), power),
    pow(temp.b(), power));
      }
}

void Image::writePPM(ostream& out)
{
   // output header
   out << "P6\n";
   out << nx << ' ' << ny << '\n';
   out << "255\n";
   int i, j;
   unsigned int ired, igreen, iblue;
   unsigned char red, green, blue;

   // output clamped [0, 255] values
   for (i = ny-1; i >= 0; i--)
      for (j = 0; j < nx; j++)
      {
 ired    = (unsigned int)(256*raster[j][i].r());
        igreen = (unsigned int)(256*raster[j][i].g());
```

```
            iblue  = (unsigned int)(256*raster[j][i].b());
            if (ired > 255) ired = 255;
            if (igreen > 255) igreen = 255;
            if (iblue > 255) iblue = 255;
            red = (unsigned char)(ired);
            green = (unsigned char)(igreen);
            blue = (unsigned char)(iblue);
            out.put(red);
            out.put(green);
            out.put(blue);
        }
}

// reads in a binary PPM
void Image::readPPM(string file_name)
{
   // open stream to file
   ifstream in;
   in.open(file_name.c_str());
   if (!in.is_open())
   {
      cerr << " ERROR -- Couldn't open file \'" << file_name << "\'.\n";
      exit(-1);
   }

   char ch, type;
   char red, green, blue;
   int i, j, cols, rows;
   int num;

   // read in header info
   in.get(ch);
   in.get(type);
   in >> cols >> rows >> num;

   nx = cols;
   ny = rows;

   // allocate raster
   raster = new rgb*[nx];
   for (i = 0; i < nx; i++)
      raster[i] = new rgb[ny];

   // clean up newline
   in.get(ch);
```

```
// store PPM pixel values in raster
for (i = ny-1; i >= 0; i--)
   for (j = 0; j < nx; j++)
   {
      in.get(red);
      in.get(green);
      in.get(blue);
      raster[j][i] =
         rgb((float)((unsigned char)red)/255.0,
             (float)((unsigned char)green)/255.0,
             (float)((unsigned char)blue)/255.0);
   }
}
```

1.8.3   Vector3 Class

A vector class is an ideal candidate for optimization since it is one of the foundations of most graphics programs. We have used aggressive inlining to avoid function call overhead and the use of const functions allow the compiler to more aggressively optimize. There are other techniques for speeding up a vector class which involve added data members, such as length, which are precomputed during initialization. We have chosen not to utilize these methods to avoid the memory overhead they incur.

```
// Vector3.h

#ifndef _VECTOR3_H_
#define _VECTOR3_H_ 1

#include <math.h>
#include <iostream.h>

class Vector3
{
public:
   Vector3() {}
   Vector3(float e0, float e1, float e2);
   Vector3(const Vector3 &v) { *this = v; }

   float x() const { return e[0]; }
   float y() const { return e[1]; }
   float z() const { return e[2]; }

   const Vector3& operator+() const;
   Vector3 operator-() const;
```

```
    float operator[](int i) const { return e[i]; }
    float& operator[](int i) { return e[i]; }

    float length() const;
    float squaredLength() const;

    void makeUnitVector();

    void setX(float _x) { e[0] = _x; }
    void setY(float _y) { e[1] = _y; }
    void setZ(float _z) { e[2] = _z; }
    float minComponent() const;
    float maxComponent() const;
    float maxAbsComponent() const;
    float minAbsComponent() const;
    int indexOfMinComponent() const;
    int indexOfMinAbsComponent() const;
    int indexOfMaxComponent() const;
    int indexOfMaxAbsComponent() const;

    friend bool operator==(const Vector3& v1, const Vector3& v2);
    friend bool operator!=(const Vector3& v1, const Vector3& v2);

    friend istream &operator>>(istream &is, Vector3 &t);
    friend ostream &operator<<(ostream &os, const Vector3 &t);

    friend Vector3 operator+(const Vector3& v1, const Vector3& v2);
    friend Vector3 operator-(const Vector3& v1, const Vector3& v2);
    friend Vector3 operator/(const Vector3& vec, float scalar);
    friend Vector3 operator*(const Vector3& vec, float scalar);
    friend Vector3 operator*(float scalar, const Vector3 &vec);

    Vector3& operator=(const Vector3& v2);
    Vector3& operator+=(const Vector3& v2);
    Vector3& operator-=(const Vector3& v2);
    Vector3& operator*=(const float t);
    Vector3& operator/=(const float t);

    friend Vector3 unitVector(const Vector3& v);
    friend Vector3 minVec(const Vector3& v1, const Vector3& v2);
    friend Vector3 maxVec(const Vector3& v1, const Vector3& v2);
    friend Vector3 cross(const Vector3 &v1, const Vector3 &v2);
    friend float dot(const Vector3& v1, const Vector3& v2);
    friend float tripleProduct(const Vector3& v1, const Vector3& v2,
const Vector3& v3);
```

```
    float e[3];
};

inline Vector3::Vector3(float e0, float e1, float e2)
{ e[0] = e0; e[1] = e1; e[2] = e2; }

inline const Vector3& Vector3::operator+() const
{ return *this; }

inline Vector3 Vector3::operator-() const
{ return Vector3(-e[0], -e[1], -e[2]); }

inline float Vector3::length() const
{ return sqrt(e[0]*e[0] + e[1]*e[1] + e[2]*e[2]); }

inline float Vector3::squaredLength() const
{ return e[0]*e[0] + e[1]*e[1] + e[2]*e[2]; }

inline void Vector3::makeUnitVector()
{ *this = *this / (*this).length(); }

inline float Vector3::minComponent() const {
    float temp = e[0];
    if (e[1] < temp) temp = e[1];
    if (e[2] < temp) temp = e[2];

    return temp;
}

inline float Vector3::maxComponent() const {
    float temp = e[0];
    if (e[1] > temp) temp = e[1];
    if (e[2] > temp) temp = e[2];

    return temp;
}

inline float Vector3::maxAbsComponent() const {
    float temp = fabs(e[0]);
    if (fabs(e[1]) > temp) temp = fabs(e[1]);
    if (fabs(e[2]) > temp) temp = fabs(e[2]);

    return temp;
}
```

```
inline float Vector3::minAbsComponent() const {
    float temp = fabs(e[0]);
    if (fabs(e[1]) < temp) temp = fabs(e[1]);
    if (fabs(e[2]) < temp) temp = fabs(e[2]);

    return temp;
}

inline int Vector3::indexOfMinComponent() const {
    int index = 0;
    float temp = e[0];
    if (e[1] < temp) { temp = e[1]; index = 1;}
    if (e[2] < temp) index = 2;

    return index;
}
inline int Vector3::indexOfMinAbsComponent() const {
    int index = 0;
    float temp = fabs(e[0]);
    if (fabs(e[1]) < temp) { temp = fabs(e[1]); index = 1; }
    if (fabs(e[2]) < temp) index = 2;

    return index;
}

inline bool operator==(const Vector3& v1, const Vector3& v2) {
    if (v1.e[0] != v2.e[0]) return false;
    if (v1.e[1] != v2.e[1]) return false;
    if (v1.e[2] != v2.e[2]) return false;
    return true;
}

inline bool operator!=(const Vector3& v1, const Vector3& v2)
{ return !(v1 == v2); }

inline int Vector3::indexOfMaxComponent() const {
    int index = 0;
    float temp = e[0];

    if (e[1] > temp) { temp = e[1]; index = 1;}
    if (e[2] > temp) index = 2;

    return index;
}
```

```
inline int Vector3::indexOfMaxAbsComponent() const {
    int index = 0;
    float temp = fabs(e[0]);
    if (fabs(e[1]) > temp) { temp = fabs(e[1]); index = 1; }
    if (fabs(e[2]) > temp) index = 2;

    return index;
}


inline Vector3 operator*(float scalar, const Vector3& vec)
{ return Vector3(vec.e[0]*scalar, vec.e[1]*scalar, vec.e[2]*scalar); }

inline Vector3 operator*(const Vector3& vec, float scalar)
{ return Vector3(vec.e[0]*scalar, vec.e[1]*scalar, vec.e[2]*scalar); }

inline Vector3 operator/(const Vector3 &vec, float scalar)
{ return Vector3(vec.e[0]/scalar, vec.e[1]/scalar, vec.e[2]/scalar); }

inline Vector3 operator+(const Vector3& v1, const Vector3& v2)
{ return Vector3(v1.e[0]+v2.e[0], v1.e[1]+v2.e[1], v1.e[2]+v2.e[2]); }

inline Vector3 operator-(const Vector3& v1, const Vector3& v2)
{ return Vector3(v1.e[0]-v2.e[0], v1.e[1]-v2.e[1], v1.e[2]-v2.e[2]); }

inline Vector3& Vector3::operator+=(const Vector3& v2) {
    *this = *this + v2;
    return *this;
}

inline Vector3& Vector3::operator=(const Vector3& v2) {
{ e[0] = v2.e[0]; e[1] = v2.e[1]; e[2] = v2.e[2]; }

inline Vector3& Vector3::operator-=(const Vector3& v2) {
    *this = *this - v2;
    return *this;
}

inline Vector3& Vector3::operator*=(float t) {
    *this = *this * t;
    return *this;
}

inline Vector3& Vector3::operator/=(float t) {
    *this = *this / t;
    return *this; }
```

```cpp
inline float dot(const Vector3 &v1, const Vector3 &v2)
{ return v1.x() * v2.x() + v1.y() * v2.y() + v1.z() * v2.z(); }

inline Vector3 cross(const Vector3 &v1, const Vector3 &v2) {
   Vector3 temp;

   temp.e[0] = v1.y() * v2.z() - v1.z() * v2.y();
   temp.e[1] = v1.z() * v2.x() - v1.x() * v2.z();
   temp.e[2] = v1.x() * v2.y() - v1.y() * v2.x();

   return temp;

}

inline Vector3 unitVector(const Vector3& v) {
   float length = v.length();
   return v / length;
}

inline Vector3 minVec(const Vector3& v1, const Vector3& v2) {
   Vector3 vec(v1);
   if (v2.x() < v1.x()) vec.setX(v2.x());
   if (v2.y() < v1.y()) vec.setY(v2.y());
   if (v2.z() < v1.z()) vec.setZ(v2.z());

   return vec;
}

inline Vector3 maxVec(const Vector3& v1, const Vector3& v2) {
   Vector3 vec(v1);
   if (v2.x() > v1.x()) vec.setX(v2.x());
   if (v2.y() > v1.y()) vec.setY(v2.y());
   if (v2.z() > v1.z()) vec.setZ(v2.z());

   return vec;
}

#endif // _VECTOR3_H_


// Vector3.cc

#include "Vector3.h"

istream &
```

```
operator>>(istream &is, Vector3 &t)
{
  float temp;
  is >> temp;
  t.e[0] = temp;
  is >> temp;
  t.e[1] = temp;
  is >> temp;
  t.e[2] = temp;

  return is;
}

ostream &
operator<<(ostream &os, const Vector3 &t)
{
  os << '('
     << t.e[0] << " "
     << t.e[1] << " "
     << t.e[2] << ')';

  return os;
}

float
tripleProduct(const Vector3 &v1, const Vector3 &v2,
      const Vector3 &v3)
{
  return dot ((cross(v1, v2)),v3);
}
```

1.8.4   Orthonormal Basis Class

```
//   ONB.h

#ifndef _ONB_H_
#define _ONB_H_ 1

#include "Vector3.h"

class ONB
{
public:
   ONB() {};
```

```
ONB(const Vector3& a, const Vector3& b, const Vector3& c)
{ U = a; V = b; W = c; }

void initFromU( const Vector3& u );
void initFromV( const Vector3& v );
void initFromW( const Vector3& w );

void set(const Vector3& a, const Vector3& b, const Vector3& c)
{ U = a; V = b; W = c; }

// Calculate the ONB from two vectors
// The first one is the Fixed vector (it is just normalized)
// The second is normalized and its direction can be adjusted
void  initFromUV( const Vector3& u, const Vector3& v );
void  initFromVU( const Vector3& v, const Vector3& u );

void  initFromUW( const Vector3& u, const Vector3& w );
void  initFromWU( const Vector3& w, const Vector3& u );

void  initFromVW( const Vector3& v, const Vector3& w );
void  initFromWV( const Vector3& w, const Vector3& v );

friend istream &operator>>(istream &is, ONB &t);
friend ostream &operator<<(ostream &os, const ONB &t);
friend bool  operator==(const ONB& o1, const ONB &o2);

// Get a component from the ONB basis
Vector3 u() const { return U; }
Vector3 v() const { return V; }
Vector3 w() const { return W; }

Vector3 U,V,W;
};

#endif // _ONB_H_



//  ONB.cc
#include "ONB.h"

#define ONB_EPSILON 0.01f

void ONB::initFromU( const Vector3& u ) {
   Vector3 n(1.0f, 0.0f, 0.0f);
   Vector3 m(0.0f, 1.0f, 0.0f);
```

```
        U = unitVector(u);
    V = cross(U, n);
    if (V.length() < ONB_EPSILON)
        V = cross(U, m);
    W = cross( U, V );
}

void  ONB::initFromV( const Vector3& v ) {
    Vector3 n(1.0f, 0.0f, 0.0f);
    Vector3 m(0.0f, 1.0f, 0.0f);

    V = unitVector(v);
    U = cross(V, n);
    if (U.squaredLength() < ONB_EPSILON)
        U = cross(V, m);
    W = cross(U, V);
}

void  ONB::initFromW( const Vector3& w ) {
    Vector3 n(1.0f, 0.0f, 0.0f);
    Vector3 m(0.0f, 1.0f, 0.0f);

    W = unitVector(w);
    U = cross(W, n);
    if (U.length() < ONB_EPSILON)
        U = cross(W, m);
    V = cross(W, U);
}

void ONB::initFromUV( const Vector3& u, const Vector3& v ) {
    U = unitVector( u );
    W = unitVector( cross(u, v) );
    V = cross( W, U);
}

void ONB::initFromVU( const Vector3& v, const Vector3& u ) {
    V = unitVector( v );
    W = unitVector( cross(u, v) );
    U = cross( V, W );
}
void ONB::initFromUW( const Vector3& u, const Vector3& w ) {
    U = unitVector( u );
    V = unitVector( cross(w, u) );
    W = cross( U, V );
}
```

```
void  ONB::initFromWU( const Vector3& w, const Vector3& u ) {
   W = unitVector( w );
   V = unitVector( cross(w, u) );
   U = cross(V, W);
}

void  ONB::initFromVW( const Vector3& v, const Vector3& w ) {
   V = unitVector( v );
   U = unitVector( cross(v, w) );
   W = cross( U, V );
}

void ONB::initFromWV( const Vector3& w, const Vector3& v ) {
   W = unitVector( w );
   U = unitVector( cross(v, w) );
   V = cross( W, U );
}

bool  operator==( const ONB & o1, const ONB & o2 )
{ return( o1.u() == o2.u() && o1.v() == o2.v() && o1.w() == o2.w()); }

istream & operator>>( istream & is, ONB & t ) {
   Vector3 new_u, new_v, new_w;
   is >> new_u >> new_v >> new_w;
   t.initFromUV( new_u, new_v );

   return is;
}

ostream & operator<<( ostream & os, const ONB & t ) {
   os << t.u() << "\n" << t.v() << "\n" << t.w() << "\n";
   return os;
}
```

1.8.5 Dynamic Array Class

This implementation grows the list by doubling the size of the base array when we run out of room. This insures that a new array does not need to be allocated to often and that the ammount of unused space in the array is never to large compared to the ammount of used space. When space usage is important the truncate function can be used to free the unused portion of the array.

```
// DynArray.h

#ifndef _DYNARRAY_H_
#define _DYNARRAY_H_ 1
```

```
// a DynArray stores data in an ordered random access structure with
// no delete operations.  Items are added with append.

template <class T> class DynArray {
public:
   DynArray();
   DynArray(int);
   ~DynArray();

   bool append(T item);             // always added to end
   bool truncate();                 // make arraySize = nData;
   void clear() { nData = 0; }
   int length() const { return nData; }
   bool empty() const { return nData == 0; }
   const T &operator[] (int i) const { return data[i]; }
   T &operator[] (int i) { return data[i]; }

   T *data;
   int nData;
   int arraySize;
};

template <class T> DynArray<T>::DynArray() {
   nData = 0;
   arraySize = 4;
   data = new T[arraySize];
}

template <class T> DynArray<T>::DynArray(int a) {
   nData = 0;
   arraySize = a;
   data = new T[arraySize];
}

template <class T> DynArray<T>::~DynArray() {
   nData = 0;
   delete [] data;
}

template <class T> bool DynArray<T>::truncate()
{
   if(nData != arraySize)
   {
      T *temp = data;
      arraySize = nData;
```

```
      if(!(data = new T[arraySize])) return false;
      for(int i = 0; i < nData; i++) data[i] = temp[i];
      delete [] temp;
   }
   return true;
}

template <class T> bool DynArray<T>::append(T item) {
   if (nData == arraySize) {
      arraySize *= 2;
      T *temp = data;
      if (!(data = new T[arraySize])) return false;
      for (int i = 0; i < nData; i++)
            data[i] = temp[i];
      delete [] temp;
   }
   data[nData++] = item;
   return true;
}
#endif // _DYN_ARRAY_H_
```

1.8.6   Random Number Generator

We only support random floats in the range $[0, 1)$ since this is almost exclusively what is used in a raytracer.

```
// RNG.h

#ifndef _RNG_H_
#define _RNG_H_ 1

class RNG
{
public:
   RNG(unsigned long long _seed = 7564231ULL)
   {
      seed      = _seed;
      mult      = 62089911ULL;
      llong_max = 4294967295ULL;
      float_max = 4294967295.0f;
   }
   float operator()();

   unsigned long long seed;
```

```
    unsigned long long mult;
    unsigned long long llong_max;
    float float_max;
};

inline float RNG::operator()()
{
    seed = mult * seed;
    return float(seed % llong_max) / float_max;
}
#endif // _RNG_H_
```

1.9 NOTES

There are a variety of profiling tools to choose from on UNIX platforms. The freeware utility *gprof* is a simple profiler that can be used on any UNIX platform. Another useful free utility is the *cvs* (www.cyclic.com) versioning system. This tool allows you to keep a version tree of your code so that you can revert to a previous version of your ray tracer at any time. It also supports code sharing among multiple developers.

The image utility *xv* (www.trilon.com/xv) is an excellent tool for converting file formats and simple image manipulations. *Adobe PhotoShop Elements* (www.adobe.com), and the free package *The Gimp* (www.gimp.org) are both powerful image manipulation utilities that should serve all of your needs.

A more complete discussion of gamma correction and other general graphics topics can be found in graphics texts such as *Fundamentals of Computer Graphics* (Shirley, A K Peters, 2002) and *3D Computer Graphics 3rd Ed.* (Watt, Addison-Wesley, 1999).

Our random number generator uses a *linear congruence algorithm.* This and other methods are discussed extensively in Knuth's classic *The Art of Computer Programming*(Addison-Wesley Publishing, 2nd, Edition, 1998).

C++ is a language that lends itself well to ray tracing. It has the object-oriented capabilities that will simplify your ray tracer but also allows low-level tweaking for speed. One drawback to C++ is that there are many hidden costs associated with classes and other C++ features. An excellent guide to avoiding these pitfalls is *Efficient C++* (Bulka and Mayhew, Addison-Wesley, 1999).

2 | Ray–Object Intersections

This chapter describes how to compute intersections between rays and objects. The general problem we are trying to solve is at what point, if any, a 3D line intersects a 3D surface. The line is always given in parametric form because that is the most convenient for ray tracing. The surface is sometimes given in implicit form and sometimes in parametric form. Solving for intersection is usually a mechanical algebraic exercise.

2.1 PARAMETRIC LINES

A line in 2D can be given in implicit form, usually $y - mx - b = 0$, or parametric form. Parametric form uses some real *parameter* to mark position on the line. For example, a parametric line in 2D might be written as

$$x(t) = 2 + 7t, \quad y(t) = 1 + 7t.$$

This would be equivalent to the explicit form $y = x - 1$.

A parametric 3D line might be written as

$$x(t) = 2 + 7t,$$
$$y(t) = 1 + 2t,$$
$$z(t) = 3 - 5t.$$

This is a cumbersome thing to write, and does not translate well to code variables, so we will write it in vector form:

$$\mathbf{p}(t) = \mathbf{o} + t\mathbf{d},$$

where, for this example, **o** and **d** are given by

$$\mathbf{o} = (2, 1, 3), \quad \mathbf{d} = (7, 2, -5).$$

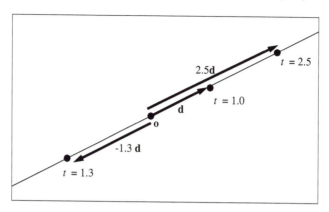

Figure 2.1. A parametric line. Note that the point **o** can be expressed as $p(0) = o + 0d$, and the point labeled $t = 2.5$ at the right can be expressed as $p(2.5) = o + 2.5d$. Every point along the line has a corresponding t value, and every value of t has a corresponding point.

The way to visualize this is to imagine that the line passes through **o** and is parallel to **d**. Given any value of t, you get some point $p(t)$ on the line. For example, at $t = 2$, $p(t) = (2, 1, 3) + 2(7, 2, -5) = (16, 5, -7)$. This general concept is illustrated in Figure 2.1.

A *line segment* can be described by a 3D parametric line and an interval $t \in [t_a, t_b]$. The line segment between two points **a** and **b** is given by $p(t) = a + t(b - a)$ with $t \in [0, 1]$. Here $p(0) = a$, $p(1) = b$, and $p(0.5) = (a + b)/2$, the midpoint between **a** and **b**.

A *ray*, or *half-line*, is a 3D parametric line with a half-open interval, usually $[0, \infty)$. We refer to all lines, line segments, and rays as "rays." This is sloppy, but corresponds to common usage, and makes the discussion simpler.

We usually want to associate a valid interval with each ray consisting of a min and max parameterization of the ray. This is useful for situations such as casting a shadow ray towards a light to test for occlusion. We want to know if the ray intersects anything between the shaded surface and the light, but not beyond the light. The interval can be a data member of the ray or passed into your intersect function as a parameter. In our implementation we use two float parameters, $tmin$ and $tmax$.

2.2 GENERAL RAY–OBJECT INTERSECTIONS

Surfaces are usually described in one of two ways: either as *implicit* equations, or *parametric* equations. This section describes standard ways to intersect rays with each type of object.

2.2.1 Implicit Surfaces

Implicit equations *implicitly* define a set of points that are on the surface

$$f(x, y, z) = 0.$$

Any point (x, y, z) that is on the surface returns zero when given as an argument to f. Any point not on the surface returns some number other than zero. This is called implicit rather than explicit because you can check whether a point is on the surface by evaluating f, but you cannot always explicitly construct a set of points on the surface. As a convenient shorthand, we will write such functions of $\mathbf{p} = (x, y, z)$ as

$$f(\mathbf{p}) = 0.$$

Given a ray $\mathbf{p}(t) = \mathbf{o} + t\mathbf{d}$ and an implicit surface $f(\mathbf{p}) = 0$, we'd like to know where they intersect. The intersection points occur when points on the ray satisfy the implicit equation

$$f(\mathbf{p}(t)) = 0.$$

This is just

$$f(\mathbf{o} + t\mathbf{d}) = 0.$$

As an example, consider the infinite plane though point **a** with surface normal **n**. The implicit equation to describe this plane is given by

$$(\mathbf{p} - \mathbf{a}) \cdot \mathbf{n} = 0.$$

Note that **a** and **n** are known quantities. The point **p** is any unknown point that satisfies the equation. If you expand this in terms of the components (x, y, z) of **p**, you will get the familiar form of the plane equation $Ax + By + Cz + D = 0$. In geometric terms, this equation says "the vector from **a** to **p** is perpendicular to the plane normal." If **p** were not in the plane, then $(\mathbf{p} - \mathbf{a})$ would not make a right angle with **n**. Plugging in the ray $\mathbf{p}(t) = \mathbf{o} + t\mathbf{d}$, we get

$$(\mathbf{o} + t\mathbf{d} - \mathbf{a}) \cdot \mathbf{n} = 0.$$

Note that the only unknown here is t. The rest of the variables are known properties of the ray or plane. If we find a t that satisfies the equation, the corresponding point $\mathbf{p}(t)$ will be a point where the line intersects the plane. Solving for t, we get

$$t = \frac{(\mathbf{a} - \mathbf{o}) \cdot \mathbf{n}}{\mathbf{d} \cdot \mathbf{n}}.$$

If we are interested only in intersections on some interval on the line, then this t must be tested to see if it is in that range. Note that there is at most one solution to the above equation, which is good because a line should hit the plane, at most, once. The case where the denominator on the right is zero corresponds to when the ray is parallel to the plane, and thus perpendicular to $\mathbf{n}$, and there is no defined intersection. When both numerator and denominator are zero, the ray is in the plane. Note that finding the intersection with implicit surfaces is often not this easy algebraically.

A surface normal, which is needed for lighting computations, is a vector perpendicular to the surface. Each point on the surface may have a different normal vector. The surface normal at the intersection point $\mathbf{p}$ is given by the gradient of the implicit function

$$\mathbf{n} = \nabla f(\mathbf{p}) = \left(\frac{\partial f(\mathbf{p})}{\partial x}, \frac{\partial f(\mathbf{p})}{\partial y}, \frac{\partial f(\mathbf{p})}{\partial z} \right).$$

The gradient vector may point "into" the surface or may point "out" from the surface.

2.2.2 Parametric Surfaces

Another way to specify 3D surfaces is with 2D *parameters*. These surfaces have the form

$$x = f(u, v),$$
$$y = g(u, v),$$
$$z = h(u, v).$$

For example, a point on the surface of the earth is given by the two parameters longitude and latitude. For example, if we put a polar coordinate system on a unit sphere with center at the origin (see Figure 2.2), we get the parametric equations

$$x = \cos \phi \sin \theta,$$
$$y = \sin \phi \sin \theta,$$
$$z = \cos \theta.$$

Ideally, we'd like to write this in vector form like the plane equation, but it isn't possible for this particular parametric form. We will return to this equation when we texture map a sphere.

To intersect a ray with a parametric surface, we set up a system of equations where the Cartesian coordinates all match:

$$o_x + td_x = f(u, v),$$
$$o_y + td_y = g(u, v),$$
$$o_z + td_z = h(u, v).$$

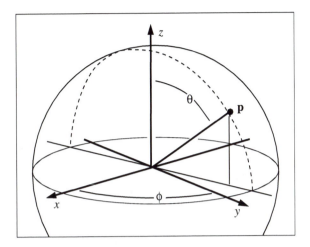

Figure 2.2. Polar coordinates on the sphere. These coordinates will be used in several places later in the book.

Here we have three equations and three unknowns (t, u, and v), so we can numerically solve for the unknowns. If we are lucky, we can solve for them analytically.

The normal vector for a parametric surface is given by

$$\mathbf{n}(u, v) = \left(\frac{\partial f}{\partial u}, \frac{\partial g}{\partial u}, \frac{\partial h}{\partial u} \right) \times \left(\frac{\partial f}{\partial v}, \frac{\partial g}{\partial v}, \frac{\partial h}{\partial v} \right).$$

2.3 RAY–SPHERE INTERSECTION

A sphere with center $\mathbf{c} = (c_x, c_y, c_z)$ and radius R can be represented by the implicit equation

$$(x - c_x)^2 + (y - c_y)^2 + (z - c_z)^2 - R^2 = 0.$$

We can write this same equation in vector form:

$$(\mathbf{p} - \mathbf{c}) \cdot (\mathbf{p} - \mathbf{c}) - R^2 = 0.$$

Again, any point $\mathbf{p}$ that satisfies this equation is on the sphere. If we plug points on the ray $\mathbf{p}(t) = \mathbf{o} + t\mathbf{d}$ into this equation we can solve for the values of t on the ray that yield points on the sphere:

$$(\mathbf{o} + t\mathbf{d} - \mathbf{c}) \cdot (\mathbf{o} + t\mathbf{d} - \mathbf{c}) - R^2 = 0.$$

Moving terms around yields

$$(\mathbf{d} \cdot \mathbf{d})t^2 + 2\mathbf{d} \cdot (\mathbf{o} - \mathbf{c})t + (\mathbf{o} - \mathbf{c}) \cdot (\mathbf{o} - \mathbf{c}) - R^2 = 0.$$

Here, everything is known but the parameter t, so this is a classic quadratic equation in t, meaning it has the form

$$At^2 + Bt + C = 0.$$

The solution to this equation is

$$t = \frac{-B \pm \sqrt{B^2 - 4AC}}{2A}.$$

Here, the term under the square root sign, $B^2 - 4AC$, is called the *discriminant* and tells us how many real solutions there are. If the discriminant is negative, its square root is imaginary and there are no intersections between the sphere and the line. If the discriminant is positive, there are two solutions: one solution where the ray enters the sphere, and one where it leaves. If the discriminant is zero, the ray grazes the sphere touching it at exactly one point. Plugging in the actual terms for the sphere and eliminating the common factors of two, we get:

$$t = \frac{-\mathbf{d} \cdot (\mathbf{o} - \mathbf{c}) \pm \sqrt{(\mathbf{d} \cdot (\mathbf{o} - \mathbf{c}))^2 - (\mathbf{d} \cdot \mathbf{d})((\mathbf{o} - \mathbf{c}) \cdot (\mathbf{o} - \mathbf{c}) - R^2)}}{(\mathbf{d} \cdot \mathbf{d})}.$$

In an actual implementation, you should first check the value of the discriminant before computing other terms. If the value of the discriminant is positive, we can then find t and determine if the intersection point is within the valid hit interval.

The normal vector at point $\mathbf{p}$ is given by the gradient $\mathbf{n} = 2(\mathbf{p} - \mathbf{c})$. The unit normal is $(\mathbf{p} - \mathbf{c})/R$.

2.4 RAY–TRIANGLE INTERSECTION

A triangle is defined by three points $\mathbf{a}$, $\mathbf{b}$ and $\mathbf{c}$. If not colinear, these points define a plane. A common way to describe this plane is with *barycentric* coordinates:

$$\mathbf{p}(\alpha, \beta, \gamma) = \alpha\mathbf{a} + \beta\mathbf{b} + \gamma\mathbf{c} \tag{2.1}$$

with the constraint

$$\alpha + \beta + \gamma = 1.$$

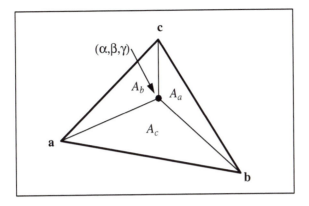

Figure 2.3. Barycentric coordinates can be found by computing the areas of subtriangles.

Barycentric coordinates seem like an abstract and unintuitive construct at first, but they turn out to be powerful and convenient. Barycentric coordinates are defined for all points on the plane. The point **p** is inside the triangle if and only if

$$0 < \alpha < 1,$$
$$0 < \beta < 1,$$
$$0 < \gamma < 1.$$

If one of the coordinates is zero, you are on an edge. If two are zero, you are at a vertex.

One way to compute barycentric coordinates is to compute the areas A_a, A_b, and A_c, of subtriangles as shown in Figure 2.3. Barycentric coordinates obey the rule

$$\alpha = A_a/A,$$
$$\beta = A_b/A,$$
$$\gamma = A_c/A,$$

where A is the area of the triangle. This rule still holds for points outside the triangle if the areas are allowed to be signed.

We can eliminate one of the variables by plugging in $\alpha = 1 - \beta - \gamma$ into Equation 2.1:

$$\mathbf{p}(\beta, \gamma) = \mathbf{a} + \beta(\mathbf{b} - \mathbf{a}) + \gamma(\mathbf{c} - \mathbf{a}).$$

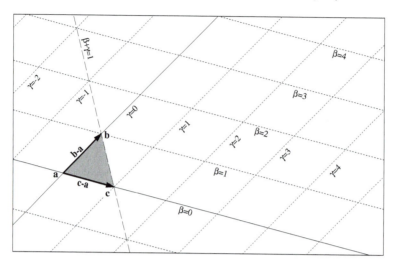

Figure 2.4. An intersection of a ray and the plane containing the triangle.

Now points are in the triangle if and only if

$$\begin{aligned} \beta + \gamma &< 1, \\ 0 &< \beta, \\ 0 &< \gamma. \end{aligned}$$

Together, β and γ parameterize a nonorthogonal coordinate system on the plane as shown in Figure 2.4.

The ray $\mathbf{p}(t) = \mathbf{o} + t\mathbf{d}$ hits the plane where

$$\mathbf{o} + t\mathbf{d} = \mathbf{a} + \beta(\mathbf{b} - \mathbf{a}) + \gamma(\mathbf{c} - \mathbf{a}). \tag{2.2}$$

This hit point is in the triangle if and only if $\beta > 0$, $\gamma > 0$, and $\beta + \gamma < 1$. A configuration where the ray hits at $(\beta, \gamma) = (1.2, 0.8)$ is shown in Figure 2.5, which is not inside the triangle as predicted by the sum of β and γ being two.

To solve for t, β, and γ in Equation 2.2, we expand it from its vector form into the three equations for the three coordinates:

$$\begin{aligned} o_x + td_x &= a_x + \beta(b_x - a_x) + \gamma(c_x - a_x), \\ o_y + td_y &= a_y + \beta(b_y - a_y) + \gamma(c_y - a_y), \\ o_z + td_z &= a_z + \beta(b_z - a_z) + \gamma(c_z - a_z). \end{aligned}$$

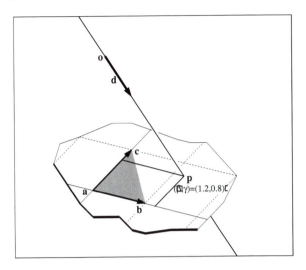

Figure 2.5. Barycentric coordinates on a plane intersected by a ray.

This can be rewritten as a standard linear equation:

$$\begin{bmatrix} a_x - b_x & a_x - c_x & d_x \\ a_y - b_y & a_y - c_y & d_y \\ a_z - b_z & a_z - c_z & d_z \end{bmatrix} \begin{bmatrix} \beta \\ \gamma \\ t \end{bmatrix} = \begin{bmatrix} a_x - o_x \\ a_y - o_y \\ a_z - o_z \end{bmatrix}.$$

The fastest classic method to solve this 3×3 linear system is *Cramer's rule*. This gives us the solutions:

$$\beta = \frac{\begin{vmatrix} a_x - o_x & a_x - c_x & d_x \\ a_y - o_y & a_y - c_y & d_y \\ a_z - o_z & a_z - c_z & d_z \end{vmatrix}}{|\mathbf{A}|},$$

$$\gamma = \frac{\begin{vmatrix} a_x - b_x & a_x - o_x & d_x \\ a_y - b_y & a_y - o_y & d_y \\ a_z - b_z & a_z - o_z & d_z \end{vmatrix}}{|\mathbf{A}|},$$

$$t = \frac{\begin{vmatrix} a_x - b_x & a_x - c_x & a_x - o_x \\ a_y - b_y & a_y - c_y & a_y - o_y \\ a_z - b_z & a_z - c_z & a_z - o_z \end{vmatrix}}{|\mathbf{A}|},$$

where the matrix $\mathbf{A}$ is

$$\mathbf{A} = \begin{bmatrix} a_x - b_x & a_x - c_x & d_x \\ a_y - b_y & a_y - c_y & d_y \\ a_z - b_z & a_z - c_z & d_z \end{bmatrix},$$

and $|\mathbf{A}|$ denotes the determinant of $\mathbf{A}$. The 3×3 determinants have common subterms that can be exploited. Looking at the linear systems with dummy variables

$$\begin{bmatrix} a & d & g \\ b & e & h \\ c & f & i \end{bmatrix} \begin{bmatrix} \beta \\ \gamma \\ t \end{bmatrix} = \begin{bmatrix} j \\ k \\ l \end{bmatrix},$$

Cramer's rule gives us

$$\beta = \frac{j(ei - hf) + k(gf - di) + l(dh - eg)}{M},$$

$$\gamma = \frac{i(ak - jb) + h(jc - al) + g(bl - kc)}{M},$$

$$t = -\frac{f(ak - jb) + e(jc - al) + d(bl - kc)}{M},$$

where

$$M = a(ei - hf) + b(gf - di) + c(dh - eg).$$

These equations can be put into code mechanically by creating variables such as *a* and *ei-minus-hf* and assuming that the compiler will (at least eventually) do its job.

The normal vector to the triangle is just a cross product of any two nonparallel vectors in the plane. By convention the points of the triangle are stored in counterclockwise order as seen from the outside of the object and thus, a (nonunit) normal vector is:

$$\mathbf{n} = (\mathbf{b} - \mathbf{a}) \times (\mathbf{c} - \mathbf{a}).$$

2.5   MORE THAN ONE OBJECT

Once you have multiple objects, you will need a routine to return the first object hit by a ray. Usually you will be only interested in hits for $t \in [t_0, t_1]$ for a ray $\mathbf{p}(t) = \mathbf{o} + t\mathbf{d}$. For example, if you are interested only in hit points "in front" of $\mathbf{o}$, that corresponds to $t \in [0, \infty)$. If you are using an object-oriented language, you should make an abstract class or interface or superclass; whatever your language calls a class, you inherit from. This class is for anything you can hit, which we will call *surface*. This class needs a routine *hit* that returns true or false for whether a ray hits it, and fills in some data (like the t value) if it returns true. Since a list of objects can be hit, the list is also a *surface* and has a hit function:

function surfacelist.hit(ray $\mathbf{o} + t\mathbf{d}$, t_0, t_1, prim)
{prim is a pointer to the object hit}
{t and prim are filled in if hit returns true}
bool hitone $\leftarrow$ false
$t \leftarrow t_1$
for all surf in list **do**
   if surf$\rightarrow$hit($\mathbf{o} + t\mathbf{d}$, t_0, t, prim) **then**
      hitone $\leftarrow$ true
return hitone

2.6 C++ CODE

2.6.1 Ray Class

```
// Ray.h
#ifndef _RAY_H_
#define _RAY_H_ 1

#include "Vector3.h"

class Ray {
public:

    Ray() {}
    Ray(const Vector3& a, const Vector3& b)
    {data[0] = a; data[1] = b;}
    Ray(const Ray& r) {*this = r;}
    Vector3 origin() const {return data[0];}
    Vector3 direction() const {return data[1];}
    Vector3 pointAtParameter(float t) const
    { return data[0] + t*data[1]; }

    Vector3 data[2];
};

inline ostream &operator<<(ostream &os, const Ray &r) {
    os << "(" << r.origin() << ") + t(" << r.direction() << ")";
    return os;
}
#endif // _RAY_H_
```

2.6.2   Shape Classes

This is a simple implementation of a shape class and a few shape types. There are many decisions to be made concerning your shape class and its virtual functions. Perhaps most important is the decision of where to perform shading calculations, such as finding the normal and UV coordinates. The most efficient approach may be to defer these calculations until you have found the nearest surface intersected. On the other hand, the normal and barycentric coordinates used for finding UV points are a by-product of some intersect routines and deferring calculations might result in doing the same work twice. Your classes may or may not want to support features such as animation and multisampling. These decisions are best left until you are sure what type of renderer you want to write. Your shape class will evolve along with the changing design of your ray tracer.

The shadowHit routine is a simple efficiency technique that takes advantage of the fact that we don't need to know any information about the occluding object. In the regular hit function we would like to pass back some information about the hit object. In order to keep the number of parameters to the hit function reasonable, we use a struct to pass back this information.

Note that in the two hit functions, we pass in a floating point time parameter. This is a time value associated with the ray we are casting into the scene. This will allow for time dependent effects we will discuss later, such as motion blur. For now, you can safely ignore the time parameter. We have included it now so that you will not have to change your virtual hit functions later.

```
// Shape.h

#ifndef _SHAPE_H_
#define _SHAPE_H_ 1

#include "Ray.h"
#include "Vector3.h"
#include "rgb.h"

class Ray;
class rgb;

struct HitRecord
{
   float t;
   Vector3 normal;
   rgb color;
};
```

```cpp
class Shape
{
public:
   virtual bool hit(const Ray& r, float tmin, float tmax, float time,
 HitRecord& record) const=0;
   virtual bool shadowHit(const Ray& r, float tmin, float tmax,
 float time) const=0;
};

#endif // _SHAPE_H_

// Triangle.h

#ifndef _TRIANGLE_H_
#define _TRIANGLE_H_ 1

#include "Shape.h"
#include "Vector3.h"
#include "rgb.h"
#include "Ray.h"

class Triangle : public Shape
{
public:
   Triangle(const Vector3& _p0, const Vector3& _p1,
       const Vector3& _p2, const rgb& _color);
   bool hit(const Ray& r, float tmin, float tmax, float time,
 HitRecord& record) const;
   bool shadowHit(const Ray& r, float tmin, float tmax,
 float time) const;

   Vector3 p0;
   Vector3 p1;
   Vector3 p2;

   rgb color;
};

#endif // _TRIANGLE_H_

// Triangle.cc

#include "Triangle.h"
Triangle::Triangle(const Vector3& _p0, const Vector3& _p1,
 const Vector3& _p2, const rgb& _color)
   : p0(_p0), p1(_p1), p2(_p2), color(_color) {}
```

```cpp
bool Triangle::hit(const Ray& r, float tmin, float tmax, float time,
    HitRecord& record)const
{
    float tval;
    float A = p0.x() - p1.x();
    float B = p0.y() - p1.y();
    float C = p0.z() - p1.z();

    float D = p0.x() - p2.x();
    float E = p0.y() - p2.y();
    float F = p0.z() - p2.z();

    float G = r.direction().x();
    float H = r.direction().y();
    float I = r.direction().z();

    float J = p0.x() - r.origin().x();
    float K = p0.y() - r.origin().y();
    float L = p0.z() - r.origin().z();

    float EIHF = E*I-H*F;
    float GFDI = G*F-D*I;
    float DHEG = D*H-E*G;

    float denom = (A*EIHF + B*GFDI + C*DHEG);

    float beta = (J*EIHF + K*GFDI + L*DHEG) / denom;

    if (beta <= 0.0f || beta >= 1.0f) return false;

    float AKJB = A*K - J*B;
    float JCAL = J*C - A*L;
    float BLKC = B*L - K*C;

    float gamma = (I*AKJB + H*JCAL + G*BLKC)/denom;
    if (gamma <= 0.0f || beta + gamma >= 1.0f) return false;

    tval = -(F*AKJB + E*JCAL + D*BLKC) / denom;
    if (tval >= tmin && tval <= tmax)
    {
        record.t = tval;
        record.normal = unitVector(cross((p1 - p0), (p2 - p0)));
        record.color  = color;
        return true;
    }
}
```

```
    return false;
}

bool Triangle::shadowHit(const Ray& r, float tmin, float tmax,
    float time)const
{
    float tval;
    float A = p0.x() - p1.x();
    float B = p0.y() - p1.y();
    float C = p0.z() - p1.z();

    float D = p0.x() - p2.x();
    float E = p0.y() - p2.y();
    float F = p0.z() - p2.z();

    float G = r.direction().x();
    float H = r.direction().y();
    float I = r.direction().z();

    float J = p0.x() - r.origin().x();
    float K = p0.y() - r.origin().y();
    float L = p0.z() - r.origin().z();

    float EIHF = E*I-H*F;
    float GFDI = G*F-D*I;
    float DHEG = D*H-E*G;

    float denom = (A*EIHF + B*GFDI + C*DHEG);

    float beta = (J*EIHF + K*GFDI + L*DHEG) / denom;

    if (beta <= 0.0f || beta >= 1.0f) return false;

    float AKJB = A*K - J*B;
    float JCAL = J*C - A*L;
    float BLKC = B*L - K*C;

    float gamma = (I*AKJB + H*JCAL + G*BLKC)/denom;
    if (gamma <= 0.0f || beta + gamma >= 1.0f) return false;

    tval =  -(F*AKJB + E*JCAL + D*BLKC) / denom;

    return (tval >= tmin && tval <= tmax);
}
```

```
//  Sphere.h

#ifndef _SPHERE_H_
#define _SPHERE_H_ 1

#include "Shape.h"
#include "Vector3.h"
#include "Ray.h"
#include "rgb.h"

class Sphere : public Shape
{
public:
   Sphere(const Vector3& _center, float _radius, const rgb& _color);
   BBox boundingBox() const;
   bool hit(const Ray& r, float tmin, float tmax, float time,
 HitRecord& record) const;
   bool shadowHit(const Ray& r, float tmin, float tmax, float time)
       const;

   Vector3 center;
   float radius;
   rgb color;
};

#endif // _SPHERE_H__


//  Sphere.cc

#include "Sphere.h"

Sphere::Sphere(const Vector3& _center, float _radius, const rgb& _color)
   : center(_center), radius(_radius), color(_color) {}

bool Sphere::hit(const Ray& r, float tmin, float tmax, float time,
     HitRecord* record)const
{
   Vector3 temp = r.origin() - center;

   double a = dot( r.direction(), r.direction() );
   double b = 2*dot( r.direction(), temp );
   double c = dot( temp, temp ) - radius*radius;

   double discriminant = b*b- 4*a*c;
```

```cpp
    // first check to see if ray intersects sphere
    if ( discriminant > 0 )
    {
       discriminant = sqrt( discriminant );
       double t = (- b - discriminant) / (2*a);

       // now check for valid interval
       if (t < tmin)
          t = (- b + discriminant) / (2*a);
       if (t < tmin || t > tmax)
          return false;

       // we have a valid hit
       rec.t = t;
       record.normal = unitVector(r.origin() + t* r.direction()
                             - center);
       record.color  = color;
       return true;
    }
    return false;
}

bool Sphere::shadowHit(const Ray& r, float tmin, float tmax,
                   float time)const
{
   Vector3 temp = r.origin() - center;

   double a = dot( r.direction(), r.direction() );
   double b = 2*dot( r.direction(), temp );
   double c = dot( temp, temp ) - radius*radius;

   double discriminant = b*b- 4*a*c;

   // first check to see if ray intersects sphere
   if ( discriminant > 0 )
   {
      discriminant = sqrt( discriminant );
      double t = (- b - discriminant) / (2*a);

      // now check for valid interval
      if (t < tmin)
         t = (- b + discriminant) / (2*a);
      if (t < tmin || t > tmax)
         return false;
```

```
    // we have a valid hit
    return true;
  }
  return false;
}
```

2.7 NOTES

If you would like to add more surface types to your ray tracer a good source
is *An Introduction to Raytracing* (edited by Glassner, Academic Press, 1989).
This book also has discussions on many other ray tracing topics still relevant to-
day. The classic paper "Distributed Ray Tracing" (Cook, Porter, and Carpenter in
Computer Graphics, Proc. SIGGRAPH '84) introduced several of the effects we
will be discussing in the advanced topics sections of future chapters. Many other
types of objects have well-studied intersection strategies. The best resource for
finding these is to look at the online *Ray Tracing News* (www.raytracingnews.com).

3 | A Simple Ray Tracer

Given the classes we have already developed, we can now create a basic ray tracing program. We first write a ray tracer that shoots one ray through each pixel and then extend this algorithm to cast many rays per pixel to improve our image quality.

3.1 A SINGLE SAMPLE RAY TRACER

We can now generate a simple image using spheres and triangles with an orthographic camera. Let's assume we have 500 by 500 pixels (i, j) numbered $(0, 0)$ through $(499, 499)$. For each pixel, generate a ray $\mathbf{r} = \mathbf{o} + t\mathbf{d}$, such that

$$\mathbf{o} = (i, j, 0),$$
$$\mathbf{d} = (0, 0, -1),$$

where the negative z direction is chosen for $\mathbf{d}$. If we chose the positive z direction, we would need to use a left-handed coordinate system, a system we would like to avoid.

Let's create a sphere with center $(250, 250, -1000)$ and radius 150, and a triangle with vertices $(300, 600, -800)$, $(0, 100, -1000)$, and $(450, 20, -1000)$. Now put these two objects into a list and for each ray, find the closest hit point. If you hit the sphere, color pixel (i, j) blue. If you hit the triangle, color it red. If you hit neither, color it dark grey. You should get an image that looks like Figure 3.1.

3.2 MULTISAMPLING

The simple ray tracer we just discussed is a single-sample ray tracer. That is, it estimates the color of a pixel by sampling the scene with one ray through the center of each pixel. This method is fast and is good for interactive applications, but it is insufficient for generating high quality images. We would like the color

Figure 3.1. Sample image for debugging with sphere and triangle and one sample per pixel. The exact parameters for this image are given in the text.

of the pixel to be an average of the colors within the pixel area. The jagged edges you see in images produced by a single-sample ray tracer, known as "jaggies," are a form of aliasing that can easily be reduced by taking multiple samples per pixel and averaging their returned colors. We accomplish this by sending a set of rays that are in some sense uniform through the pixel, and then averaging the colors seen along these rays.

To estimate the average color for the area of a pixel, we need to establish a 2D coordinate system on the pixels. We use the coordinate system shown in

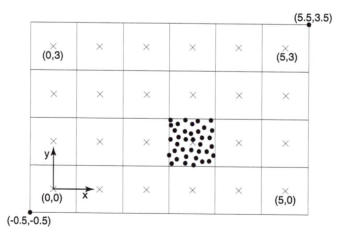

Figure 3.2. The screen coordinates used for sampling pixels. Pixel centers are exact integers. A set of area samples are shown for pixel $(3, 1)$.

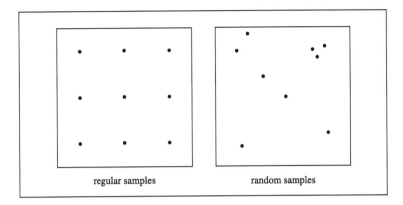

Figure 3.3. Examples of regular and random samples with nine samples per pixel.

Figure 3.2 with pixel centers on an integer lattice. To compute the average color of a pixel, we average the color at many points within the pixel. For pixel $(3, 1)$, these samples are in the area where $2.5 \leq x \leq 3.5$ and $0.5 \leq y \leq 1.5$. For such restriction, we use the set notation $(x, y) \in [2.5, 3.5] \times [0.5, 1.5]$.

This sampling technique to estimate the average color of a pixel is known as *Monte Carlo integration*. Monte Carlo integration is simply the method of estimating an integral by randomly sampling the solution space of the integral and taking the mean of the results. In later chapters we will examine this technique more formally, but for now we can implement using our intuition of an average.

3.2.1   Sampling Methods

To actually compute an estimate of the average color within a pixel, we need to have an algorithm for picking "uniform" points on the pixel. There are several methods of obtaining samples within a pixel. Typically, such algorithms pick samples $(x, y) \in [0, 1] \times [0, 1]$ and then add $(i - 0.5, j - 0.5)$ to the (x, y) values to move them to cover the pixel areas. Two simple possibilities for generating samples on the unit square are shown in Figure 3.3. It would be easy enough to simply use a random number generator to choose random points within a unit square. We can then map these values to the current pixel.

The problem with random sampling is that if we are unlucky, a given set of samples may be bunched together within the unit square. This will give an inaccurate estimate of the pixel's average color since we are using many samples within a small area of the pixel to estimate the whole pixel. We would rather have our samples more uniformly distributed over the unit square. One method to avoid clumping is to choose our samples as the vertices of a uniform grid within the unit square. An additional benefit is that computation is reduced as a result of the fact that the sample pattern only needs to be generated once for an entire image. This is because the same pattern is used for all pixels. Unfortunately, regular sampling suffers from a new flaw. Aliasing can occur as a result of the correlation of samples between pixels. There are many sampling schemes that attempt to have the good aspects of regular and random sampling. Some of these are shown in Figure 3.4.

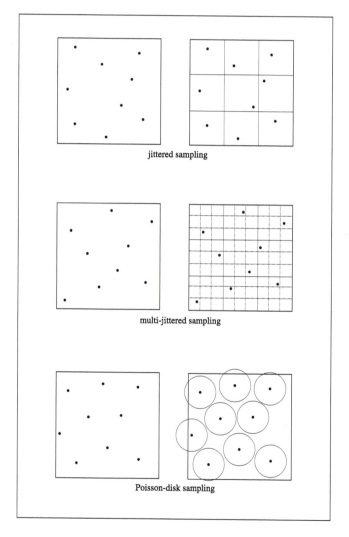

Figure 3.4. Examples of sample patterns generated by different strategies for nine samples per pixel.

One sampling method that ensures that samples are well distributed in x and in y is *n-rooks* sampling. This method is analagous to placing n rooks on an n by n chessboard in such a way that no rook is attacking another. This is done by placing the rooks along any diagonal of the chessboard and then shuffling the x coordinates of the pieces. This method is excellent for estimating integrals in which most of the variation is parallel to the vertical and/or the horizontal axes. A drawback is that not all solutions to the n-rooks problem are well distibuted across the unit square; for instance, placing all samples along a single diagonal.

The most commonly used form of sampling chooses samples by dividing the unit square into a grid of n bins and choosing a sample randomly within each bin. This is known as *jittered* or *stratified* sampling. Now we have the nicely distributed samples of regular sampling without the correlation between pixels. The importance of using stratification when sampling in a ray tracer cannot be overstated. Using finite sampling to estimate an integral, such as the average color over the area of a pixel, is a technique which is used in many different ray tracing problems. Stratifying over the sample space gives more visually pleasing results than random sampling in almost all cases. The exception is when the dimensionality of the sample space is high, in which case there is not much to be gained from stratification.

A method that combines the advantages of both jittered and n-rooks sampling is *multijittering*. There is a subset of n-rooks solutions which are also jittered in a *square root of n* by *square root of n* grid. Now we have the benefits of jittering along with a nice vertical and horizontal distribution.

Poisson-disk sampling takes random samples sequentially, rejecting them if they are within a threshold distance of any previously accepted samples.

3.2.2 Filtering Methods

Improving image quality by uniformly averaging colors over the pixel area is known as *box filtering*. Box filtering can produce much better images than point sampling the center of the pixel. Figure 3.5 demonstrates this by sampling the function:

$$L(x,y) = \frac{1}{2}\left(1 + \sin\left(\frac{x^2+y^2}{100}\right)\right)$$

in screen space over a 512 by 384 image. Note that this is a 2D function defined for sample locations in screen space, so it is evaluated directly instead of tracing rays. While the severe false patterns here are not likely to arise in real 3D scenes, smaller versions of the effect are common, and they are particularly severe in dynamic environments.

Figure 3.5. Top: Single sample at the center of each pixel. Bottom: Box filter.

Figure 3.6. Top: Tent filter. Bottom: Cubic b-spline filter.

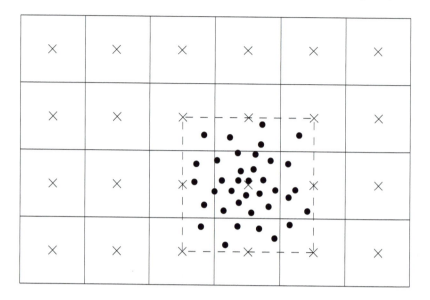

Figure 3.7. n can be used to create a estimate for pixel color.

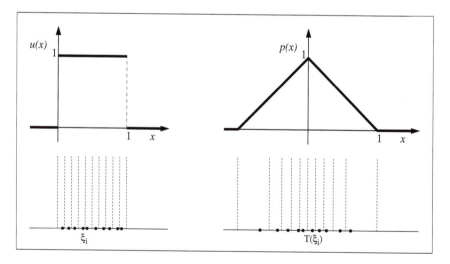

Figure 3.8. We can take a set of canonical random samples and transform them to nonuniform samples.

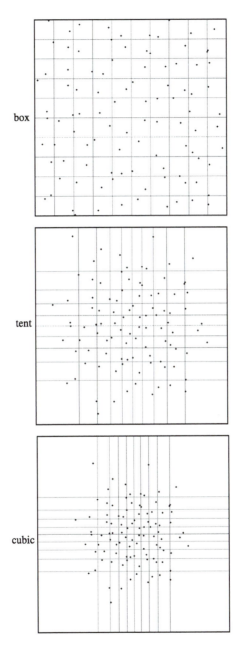

Figure 3.9. The same jittered pattern (top) sent through warping filters for tent (middle) and cubic (bottom) figures. Note that although the squares are shown the same size, the x and y coordinates are in the ranges $[0, 1]$, $[-1, 1]$, and $[-2, 2]$, respectively.

In addition to box filtering, we can try using a nonuniformly distributed filtering to improve our estimates. This allows us to give higher importance to samples nearer the center of the pixel. Figure 3.6 shows tent and cubic spline filters for our test function. Notice that the false patterns (aliasing) diminishes for the higher-order filters.

There are two basic strategies we can employ to do this. The first method is to give each sample a weight based on the importance of its location. The alternative is to nonuniformly distribute the samples according to the filter weighting. This way, each sample has the same weight but there will be more samples in the areas of higher importance. The latter nonuniform technique is illustrated in Figure 3.7.

A simple improvement over box filtering is a tent filter. The tent filter gives a weighting corresponding to a linear b-spline function. The area close to the center of the pixel is weighted heavily and the weighting decreases linearly with vertical and horizontal distance from the pixel center. The way we generate sample values with the desired distribution is to "warp" uniform samples by passing them through some function f from [0,1] to [-1,1]:

$$x = f(x),$$
$$y = f(y).$$

This way stratified samples can stay stratified while being nonuniform as shown in Figure 3.8. The result of passing samples through warping functions for tent and cubic filters is shown in Figure 3.9. Code for the warping functions is given at the end of this chapter.

3.3   C++ CODE

3.3.1   Single Sample Orthogonal Viewing Ray Tracer

Here is an implementation of the ray tracer described in Section 1. This program will be a good test for most of the classes you have written so far. The resulting image using the given geometry should look like Figure 3.1.

```
//  main.cc

#include <vector>
#include <iostream>
#include "Vector3.h"
#include "rgb.h"
#include "Image.h"
#include "Shape.h"
#include "Triangle.h"
```

```cpp
#include "Sphere.h"
using namespace std;

int
main()
{
    HitRecord rec;
    bool is_a_hit;
    float tmax;                  // max valid t parameter
    Vector3 dir(0, 0, -1);       // direction of viewing rays

    // geometry
    vector<Shape*> shapes;
    shapes.push_back( new Sphere(Vector3(250, 250, -1000), 150,
                            rgb(.2, .2, .8)) );
    shapes.push_back( new Triangle(Vector3(300.0f, 600.0f, -800),
                            Vector3(0.0f, 100.0f, -1000),
                            Vector3(450.0f, 20.0f, -1000),
                            rgb(.8, .2, .2)) );

    Image im(500, 500);

    // loop over pixels
    for (int i = 0; i < 500; i++)
        for (int j = 0; j < 500; j++)
        {
            tmax = 100000.0f;
            is_a_hit = false;
            Ray r(Vector3(i, j, 0), dir);

            // loop over list of Shapes
            for(int k = 0; k < shapes.size(); k++)
                if (shapes[k]->hit(r, .00001f, tmax, rec))
                {
                    tmax = rec.t;
                    is_a_hit = true;
                }

            if (is_a_hit)
                im.set(i, j, rec.color);
            else
                im.set(i, j, rgb(.2, .2, .2));
        }
    im.writePPM(cout);
}
```

3.3.2 Sample Class

This is a sampling class which decouples the sampling and filtering methods so we can mix and match them in any way.

```cpp
// Sample.h

#ifndef _SAMPLE_H_
#define _SAMPLE_H_

class Vector2;

// 2D sampling
void random(Vector2* samples, int num_samples);
// jitter assumes num_samples is a perfect square
void jitter(Vector2* samples, int num_samples);
void nrooks(Vector2* samples, int num_samples);
// multiJitter assumes num_samples is a perfect square
void multiJitter(Vector2* samples, int num_samples);
void shuffle(Vector2* samples, int num_samples);

void boxFilter(Vector2* samples, int num_samples);
void tentFilter(Vector2* samples, int num_samples);
void cubicSplineFilter(Vector2* samples, int num_samples);

// 1D sampling
void random(float* samples, int num_samples);
void jitter(float* samples, int num_samples);
void shuffle(float* samples, int num_samples);

// helper function for cubicSplineFilter
inline float solve(float r) {
   float u = r;
   for (int i = 0; i < 5; i++)
      u = (11.0f * r + u * u *(6.0f + u *(8.0f - 9.0f * u))) /
 (4.0f + 12.0f * u * (1.0f + u * (1.0f - u)));
   return u;
}

// helper function for cubicSplineFilter
inline float cubicFilter(float x) {
   if (x < 1.0f / 24.0f)
      return pow(24 * x, 0.25f) - 2.0f;
   else if (x < 0.5)
      return solve(24.0f * (x - 1.0f / 24.0f) / 11.0f) - 1.0f;
   else if (x < 23.0f / 24.0f)
      return 1.0f - solve(24.0f * (23.0f / 24.0f - x) / 11.0f);
   else
      return 2 - pow(24.0f * (1.0f-x), 0.25f);
}
#endif // _SAMPLE_H

// Sample.cc

#include "Sample.h"
#include "Vector2.h"
#include <math.h>
```

```cpp
#include <stdlib.h>

void random(Vector2* samples, int num_samples)
{
   for (int i = 0; i < num_samples; i++)
   {
      samples[i].setX(drand48());
      samples[i].setY(drand48());
   }
}

// assumes num_samples is a perfect square
void jitter(Vector2* samples, int num_samples)
{
   int sqrt_samples = (int)(sqrt(num_samples));
   for(int i = 0; i < sqrt_samples; i++)
      for(int j = 0; j < sqrt_samples; j++)
      {
         float x = ((double)i + drand48()) / (double)sqrt_samples;
         float y = ((double)j + drand48()) / (double)sqrt_samples;
         (samples[i*sqrt_samples +j]).setX(x);
         (samples[i*sqrt_samples +j]).setY(y);
      }
}

void nrooks(Vector2* samples, int num_samples)
{
   for (int i = 0; i < num_samples; i++)
   {
      samples[i].setX(((double)i + drand48()) / (double)num_samples);
      samples[i].setY(((double)i + drand48()) / (double)num_samples);
   }
   // shuffle the x coords
   for (int i = num_samples - 2; i >= 0; i--)
   {
      int target = int(drand48() * (double)i);
      float temp = samples[i+1].x();
      samples[i+1].setX(samples[target].x());
      samples[target].setX(temp);
   }
}

// assumes num_samples is a perfect square
void multiJitter(Vector2* samples, int num_samples)
{
   int sqrt_samples = (int)sqrt(num_samples);
   float subcell_width = 1.0f/(float(num_samples));

   // Initialize points to the "canonical" multi-jittered pattern
   for (int i = 0; i < sqrt_samples; i++)
      for (int j = 0; j < sqrt_samples; j++)
      {
```

```
            samples[i*sqrt_samples + j].e[0] =
                i*sqrt_samples*subcell_width +
                j*subcell_width + drand48() * subcell_width;
            samples[i*sqrt_samples + j].e[1] =
                j*sqrt_samples*subcell_width +
                i*subcell_width + drand48() * subcell_width;
        }

    // shuffle x coords within each column and y coords within each row
    for (int i = 0; i < sqrt_samples; i++)
        for (int j = 0; j < sqrt_samples; j++)
        {
            int k = j + int(drand48() * (sqrt_samples - j - 1));
            float t = samples[i*sqrt_samples + j].e[0];
            samples[i*sqrt_samples + j].e[0] = samples[i*sqrt_samples + k].e[0];
            samples[i*sqrt_samples + k].e[0] = t;

            k = j + int(drand48() * (sqrt_samples - j - 1));
            t = samples[j*sqrt_samples + i].e[1];
            samples[j*sqrt_samples + i].e[1] = samples[k*sqrt_samples + i].e[1];
            samples[k*sqrt_samples + i].e[1] = t;
        }
}


void shuffle(Vector2* samples, int num_samples)
{
    for (int i = num_samples - 2; i >= 0; i--)
    {
        int target = int(drand48() * (double)i);
        Vector2 temp = samples[i+1];
        samples[i+1] = samples[target];
        samples[target] = temp;
    }
}


void boxFilter(Vector2* samples, int num_samples)
{
    for (int i = 0; i < num_samples; i++)
    {
        samples[i].setX(samples[i].x() - 0.5f);
        samples[i].setY(samples[i].y() - 0.5f);
    }
}


void tentFilter(Vector2* samples, int num_samples)
{
    for (int i = 0; i < num_samples; i++)
    {
        float x = samples[i].x();
        float y = samples[i].y();

        if (x < 0.5f) samples[i].setX((float)sqrt(2.0*(double)x) - 1.0f);
        else samples[i].setX(1.0f - (float)sqrt(2.0 - 2.0 * (double)x));
```

```
        if (y < 0.5f) samples[i].setY((float)sqrt(2.0*(double)y) - 1.0f);
        else samples[i].setY(1.0f - (float)sqrt(2.0 - 2.0 * (double)y));
    }
}

void cubicSplineFilter(Vector2* samples, int num_samples)
{
    for (int i = 0; i < num_samples; i++)
    {
        float x = samples[i].x();
        float y = samples[i].y();

        samples[i].e[0] = cubicFilter(x);
        samples[i].e[1] = cubicFilter(y);
    }
}

void random(float* samples, int num_samples)
{
    for (int i = 0; i < num_samples; i++)
        samples[i] = drand48();
}

void jitter(float* samples, int num_samples)
{
    for (int i = 0; i < num_samples; i++)
        samples[i] = ((double)i + drand48()) / (double)num_samples;
}

void shuffle(float* samples, int num_samples)
{
    for (int i = num_samples - 2; i >= 0; i--)
    {
        int target = int(drand48() * (double)i);
        float temp = samples[i+1];
        samples[i+1] = samples[target];
        samples[target] = temp;
    }
}
```

3.4 NOTES

Later in the book we describe other effects which are made possible through multisampling. The classic paper "Distributed Ray Tracing" (Cook, Porter, and Carpenter, *SIGGRAPH Proceedings of the 11th Annual Conference on Computer Graphics and Interactive Techniques*, 1984) gives a principled discussion of these techniques.

A nice discussion of QMC sampling is given in "Quasi-Monte Carlo Methods in Computer Graphics, Part I and II" (Keller and Heidrich, *Technical*

Report 242/94, University of Kaiserslautern). For a complete discussion of the interleaved sampling technique see the paper "Interleaved Sampling" (Keller and Heidrich, *Rendering Techniques 2001*, edited by Gortler and Myszkowski, Springer-Verlag, 2001).

Higher order spline filters are discussed in the article "Generation of Stratified Samples for B-Spline Pixel Filtering" (Stark and Shirley, *Journal of Graphics Tools*, to appear). Our implementation of a cubic B-spline filter is based on this paper.

4 | Viewing

The simplest image aquisition device we can make is a *pinhole camera*. We just take a box painted black on the inside, poke a hole on one side, and tape film to the inside of the opposite side (Figure 4.1). At a given point on the film, only light from a certain direction will reach it, so the exposure of the film is proportional to the light seen in that direction. In this chapter, we simulate such a device. In real life pinhole cameras are rarely used because a long exposure time is needed for cameras with small pinholes, and the image is blurry for large pinholes. Instead, a large hole (aperture) is used and a lens is put in it. Now the color at a point on the film is that gathered from a cone of directions. We will simulate one of these lens-based cameras as well using a *thin-lens* approximation. Finally, we will account for the fact that in real cameras, there is a nonzero exposure time in which objects move, causing *motion blur* effects.

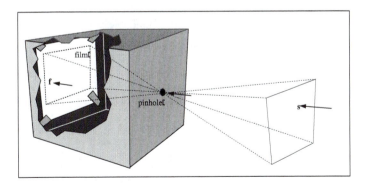

Figure 4.1. A real pinhole camera. Light enters the pinhole from a specific direction and exposes a particular part of the film. The film will capture a scene in sharp focus, but it requires significant exposure time. The color of light at point **s** in the direction shown will stay the same as it passes through the pinhole, and as it hits the film at **f**.

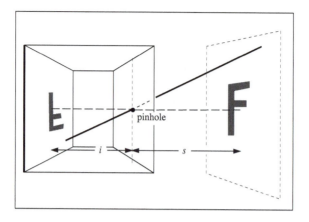

Figure 4.2. An image passing through a rectangle at distance s will be mapped onto the film.

4.1 AXIS-ALIGNED VIEWING

We can implement a synthetic version of a pinhole camera. A nice thing is that we can create a virtual film plane *in front* of the camera and forget that the film is behind the pinhole. To do this, we need to set up a projection of the film out in space. This is shown in Figure 4.2. Note that the selection of the distance s is arbitrary; if we make it bigger the rectangle and the image grow, and the same image will be saved. Many renderers set $s = 1$ for simplicity, but we will use a variable s when we get to cameras with lenses later in this chapter.

To implement the camera, we pick a specific rectangle aligned to our viewing system as shown in Figure 4.3. The viewing system has center **e** which is defined to be the origin in uvw coordinates and is aligned to the **uvw** basis. In uvw coordinates, the diagonal corners of the rectangle is given by (u_0, v_0) and (u_1, v_1). The point **c** is the lower left-hand corner of the rectangle, and the vectors **a** and **b** run along the bottom and left sides of the rectangle. These are:

$$\mathbf{a} = (u_1 - u_0)\mathbf{u}$$
$$\mathbf{b} = (v_1 - v_0)\mathbf{v}$$
$$\mathbf{c} = u_0\mathbf{u} + v_0\mathbf{v} - s\mathbf{w}.$$

Note that the rectangle need not be centered on the gaze direction (so it is not required that $u_0 = -u_1$). The rectangle is in the negative **w** direction because we want to both maintain a right-handed coordinate system, and have **u** go to the right on the rectangle. To separate pixel coordinates and the camera, we assume a $[0, 1]^2$ coordinate system on the window, where the coordinates are (a, b).

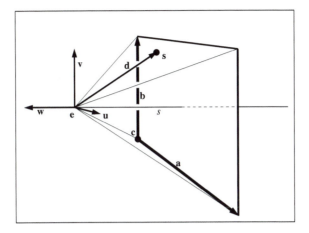

Figure 4.3. The viewing rectangle is a distance s from **e** along the negative **w** axis, and is parallel to the **uv** plane.

A point **s** on the screen is just:

$$\mathbf{s} = \mathbf{c} + a\mathbf{a} + b\mathbf{b}.$$

The ray from **e** to **s** is then:

$$\mathbf{e} + t(\mathbf{s} - \mathbf{e}).$$

To go from pixel coordinates (x, y) to (a, b), we map $[-0.5, n_x - 0.5]$ to $[0, 1]$ and $[-0.5, n_y - 0.5]$ to $[0, 1]$:

$$a = \frac{x + 0.5}{n_x},$$

$$b = \frac{y + 0.5}{n_y}.$$

4.2   SETTING VIEW PARAMETERS

If we want to have an axis-aligned view from the origin, we can use just the ray above as xyz coordinates. However, we usually like to be able to set view location and orientation. There are many ways to do this, but we will describe the common one shown in Figure 4.4.

The variables that are specified are:

- **e**, the xyz eyepoint (pinhole);

- **g**, the xyz direction of gaze (this is also the normal to the viewing rectangle, so it is sometimes called the *view-plane normal*);

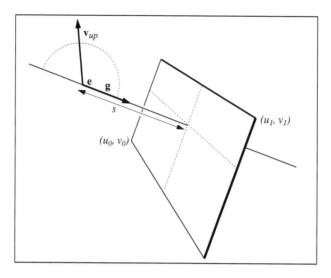

Figure 4.4. Viewing from an arbitrary position.

- $\mathbf{v}_{\text{up}}$, the *view-up vector* (this is any vector in the plane of the gaze direction $\mathbf{g}$ and the vector pointing out of the top of the head);

- s, the distance from $\mathbf{e}$ to the viewing rectangle;

- u_0, v_0, u_1, v_1, the uv coordinates of the rectangle corners.

From this information we can establish an aligned uvw frame where $\mathbf{e}$ is the origin and the basis vectors are

$$\mathbf{w} = -\frac{\mathbf{g}}{\|\mathbf{g}\|},$$
$$\mathbf{u} = \frac{\mathbf{v}_{\text{up}} \times \mathbf{w}}{\|\mathbf{v}_{\text{up}} \times \mathbf{w}\|},$$
$$\mathbf{v} = \mathbf{w} \times \mathbf{u}.$$

Note that this is a general viewing system, so some care must be taken in setting parameters. If you want the viewing rectangle centered around the gaze direction, make sure $u_0 = -u_1$ and $v_0 = -u_1$. If you want to have square pixels, make sure that

$$\frac{u_1 - u_0}{v_1 - v_0} = \frac{n_x}{n_y}.$$

Finally, note that although s is arbitrary as long as it is positive, the bigger it is the bigger the window height and width have to be to get the same image. The

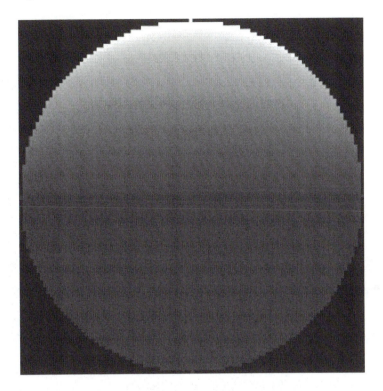

Figure 4.5. A sample use of viewing parameters.

ratio of $v_1 - v_0$ to $2s$ is the tangent of half of the "vertical field-of-view." This is another way to fix some viewing parameters.

One nice thing about not requiring the viewing rectangle to be centered around the gaze direction is that you can run different "tiles" of a single image in concurrently running programs and then join them together for a lazy programmer's parallel code. You can also generate stereo images with proper eye separation; neither eye is centered on the screen if the nose is.

An example is shown in Figure 4.5 with parameters $\mathbf{e} = (0, 0, 2)$, $\mathbf{v}_{up} = (0, 1, 0)$, $\mathbf{g} = (0, 0, -2)$, $(u_0, v_0) = (-2, -2)$, $(u_1, v_1) = (2, 2)$, $s = 2$, $n_x = n_y = 101$, and a sphere with center $(0, 0, 0)$, radius $\sqrt{2}$, and color set to 0.1 plus 0.9 times the dot product of the surface normal and a unit vector in the y direction.

Note that you could change $\mathbf{g}$ to anything with a positive y component and a zero x component and the image won't change. Change $\mathbf{v}_{up}$ to point in the $\mathbf{x}$ direction and the image should rotate 90 degrees. Decrease s and the sphere should look smaller.

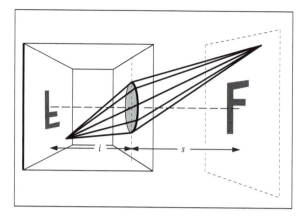

Figure 4.6. For four samples, stratified samples on the lens are randomly paired with stratified samples on the pixel.

4.3 THIN-LENS CAMERAS

A pinhole camera creates images where everything is in perfect focus. For images with *depth-of-field*, where some objects are not in focus, we use a *thin-lens* camera model. Such a model is easy to implement in a ray tracer.

A thin-lens camera replaces the pinhole with a disk-shaped "thin-lens," which has certain idealized behavior (Figure 4.6). If the camera is focused on a point at distance s from the lens, all light from that point will be focused at a point distance i behind the lens. These two points will both lie along a line through the lens center. The distances i and s obey the *thin-lens law*:

$$\frac{1}{s} + \frac{1}{i} = \frac{1}{f}.$$

Here f is the focal length of the camera. In a normal camera, f is a few centimeters and as can be seen from the formula, s cannot be smaller than f since i must be positive.

If we just want focusing effects and do not need to match a specific real camera, we can just specify the s at which objects will be in perfect focus, and the radius R of the lens. Remarkably, the only thing that changes from our pinhole camera is that s is no longer arbitrary, and the ray origin $\mathbf{q}$ is randomly chosen from a disk of radius R in the uv plane centered at $\mathbf{e}$ (Figure 4.7). In practice, the random point chosen has no effect when an object is at distance s from the lens. When an object is not at s, the rays from different points on the lens will hit the object in different places, causing a blurred appearance when many ways are averaged. So the distance s is much like the distance on a real camera's focusing

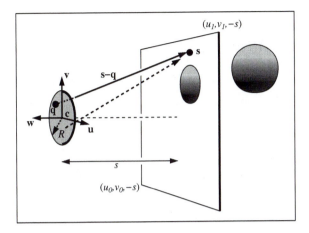

Figure 4.7. Rays from all points on the lens will go toward the same point **s** on the plane of perfect focus.

mechanism; objects at that distance will be in focus, and objects nearer or father than s will be blurry.

To mimic a real camera, we specify a film size (W, H) and focal length f. The film size is the actual physical size of the film that gets exposed—so H is approximately the distance between the sprockets on 35 mm film. Then we can specify where we are focusing on $s > f$. To specify the aperture of the lens we could just specify R, but the tradition is to use the perhaps less obvious *f-number*, $\mathbf{N} = f/(2R)$. Given these variables, we have

$$\frac{u_1}{W/2} = \frac{v_1}{H/2} = \frac{s}{i}.$$

We know that

$$i = \frac{sf}{s - f},$$

and

$$(u_1, v_1) = (-u_0, -v_0) = \left(\frac{W}{2} \frac{(s - f)}{f}, \frac{H}{2} \frac{(s - f)}{f} \right).$$

For a typical 35 mm camera and lens, $f = 50$ mm, $W = 36$ mm, and $H = 24$ mm. Images for a camera with f-number 5.6 are shown in Figure 4.8. Changing the focus is shown in Figure 4.9.

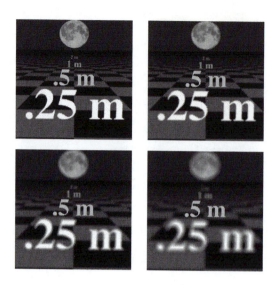

Figure 4.8. Cameras with f-numbers 22, 11, 5.6, and 3.3 focused at 0.5 meters. Images courtesy of Mike Stark.

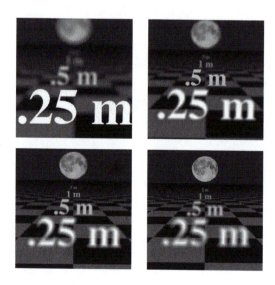

Figure 4.9. Camera with f-number 5.6 varying the focus. Images courtesy of Mike Stark.

4.4 MOTION BLUR

When a camera takes a picture, the shutter is open for a small interval of time. What happens when an object being photographed is moving quickly relative to shutter speed? A point on the film plane may see the object for part of the shutter's open time and then see the backgrond behind it for the rest of the interval. This is the cause of motion blur. Motion blur not only allows us to create realistic still frames of objects in motion, but is also critical for animations.

We can simulate this effect within a multisampling ray tracer by defining the location of an object as a function of time and associating a random time value with each ray. The ray's time will be uniformly random between T_{open} and T_{close}, the times when the shutter of the camera are opened and closed. An example is shown in Figure 4.10.

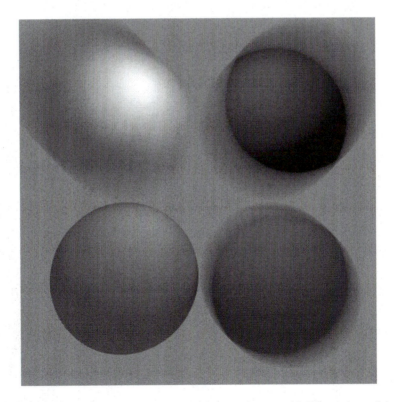

Figure 4.10. An example of motion blur created by generating rays with different times. Spheres have center positions that vary with time. The sphere on the lower left is stationary and the rest have varying velocities.

4.5 MULTIDIMENSIONAL SAMPLING

Recall that each ray has a random point on a pixel as its target. To add a thin-lens camera with motion blur, each ray must also have a random origin on the lens and a random time. One way to implement this is to take five random numbers $(\xi_0, \xi_1, \xi_2, \xi_3, \xi_4)$ in $[0, 1)^5$ and use the first two coordinates to seed the lens sampling, the next two for the pixel sampling, and the last for time. However, we saw before that in 2D for pixel antialiasing, jittering was much better than pure random sampling in terms of reducing noise as the number of samples increased. So is there some way to keep the benefits of jittering for these five dimensional samples? The obvious (and very bad) approach is to divide the 5D cube intro jittering bins and place samples there. For example we could take 32 samples in a 2 by 2 by 2 by 2 by 2 cube. While this is jittered in 5D, note that in pixel space our sampling is poor; there would be four bins each with 8 samples that are random within that bin. So if we ran our ray tracer with non-moving objects and a very small aperture, our antialiasing would be worse than that of the last chapter in that more noise would be apparent.

Let's ignore the lens sampling for now and examine the motion-blur computation. Perhaps we can use part of the n-rooks idea from the previous chapter. That strategy works better for jittering when the edges in a pixel are primarily horizontal or vertical. If we assume most variation in pixels is either due to edges or motion, that sort of separation is true for the 2D pixel samples and the 1D time samples. So for four samples, we could generate four jittered 2D samples and four 1D jittered samples and randomly pair them to create 3D samples that are well distributed in the first two dimensions as well as the last dimension (Figure 4.11). The same idea could be done with pixel and lens samples in 4D (Figure 4.12).

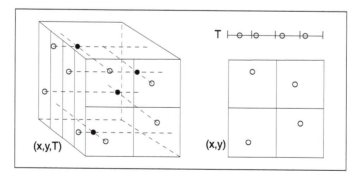

Figure 4.11. To generate pixel/time samples, we stratify in space and time so that the projections on the pixel and in time are well-distributed.

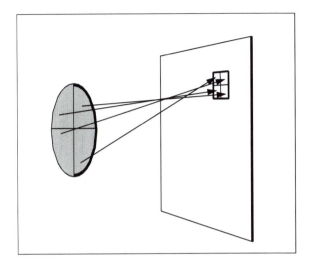

Figure 4.12. For four samples, stratified samples on the lens are randomly paired with stratified samples on the pixel.

For the full 5D case we can create a good set of 2D samples for the pixel, another set of 2D samples for the lens, and a good set of 1D samples for time. The samples for a four sample pixel with lens and time sampling are shown in Figure 4.13.

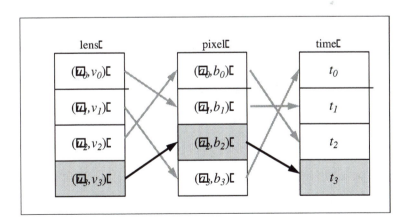

Figure 4.13. The dark-shaded path represents a set of sample seeds that generates one ray. Note that each column is a set of 2D or 1D stratified samples.

4.6   C++ CODE

4.6.1   Camera Class

Here is a straightforward camera implementation. For simplicity, we have used a
square lens rather than a disk-shaped lens.

```cpp
// Camera.h

#ifndef _CAMERA_H_
#define _CAMERA_H_

#include "Ray.h"
#include "ONB.h"

class Camera
{
public:
   Camera() {}
   Camera(const Camera& orig)
   {
       center = orig.center;
       corner = orig.corner;
       across = orig.across;
       up     = orig.up;
       uvw    = orig.uvw;
       u0     = orig.u0;
       u1     = orig.u1;
       v0     = orig.v0;
       v1     = orig.v1;
       d      = orig.d;
       lens_radius = orig.lens_radius;

   }


   Camera(Vector3 c, Vector3 gaze, Vector3 vup, float aperture, float left,
   float right, float bottom, float top, float distance)
       : center(c), d(distance), u0(left), u1(right), v0(bottom), v1(top)
       {
   lens_radius = aperture/2.0F;
   uvw.initFromWV( -gaze, vup );
   corner = center + u0*uvw.u() + v0*uvw.v() - d*uvw.w();
   across = (u0-u1)*uvw.u();
   up = (v0-v1)*uvw.v();
       }
```

```
    // a and b are the pixel positions
    // xi1 and xi2 are the lens samples in the range (0, 1)^2
    Ray getRay(float a, float b, float xi1, float xi2)
    {
        Vector3 origin = center + 2.0F*(xi1-0.5F)*lens_radius*uvw.u() +
2.0F*(xi2-0.5F)*lens_radius*uvw.v();
        Vector3 target = corner + across*a + up*b;
        return Ray(origin, unitVector(target-origin));
    }

    Vector3 center, corner, across, up;
    ONB uvw;
    float lens_radius;
    float u0, u1, v0, v1;
    float d;
};

#endif // _CAMERA_H_
```

4.6.2 Dynamic Sphere Class

DynSphere uses a time dependent function to determine its center location. You will need to add a time parameter to your shape class virtual hit function in order to use this class. The real time is then linearly interpolated between mintime and maxtime using this value. Shapes that are not dynamic will simply ignore this parameter. The motion of this sphere is just a straight line. Since the motion is procedurally defined you can use any arbitrary equation to determine the center of the sphere. The most flexible approach would be to have the constructor of your DynSphere class take a pointer to a getCenter function so each sphere could have different motions. If you wanted the sphere to spin as well as translate, you should add an *up* vector to the sphere which would be rotated with a time-dependent transform in the getCenter function.

```
// DynSphere.h

#ifndef _DYN_SPHERE_H_
#define _DYN_SPHERE_H_

#include "Shape.h"
#include "Vector3.h"
#include "Ray.h"
#include "rgb.h"

class DynSphere : public Shape
```

```
{
public:
    DynSphere(const Vector3& _ocenter, float _radius,
        const rgb& _color, float mintime, float maxtime);
    bool hit(const Ray& r, float tmin, float tmax, float time,
 HitRecord& record)const;
    bool shadowHit(const Ray& r, float tmin, float tmax, float time)
    const; Vector3 getCenter(float time)const;

    Vector3 ocenter;
    float mintime;
    float maxtime;
    float radius;
    rgb color;
};


#endif // _DYN_SPHERE_H__


// DynSphere.cc

#include "DynSphere.h"

DynSphere::DynSphere(const Vector3& _ocenter, float _radius,
const rgb& _color, float min_time, float max_time)
: ocenter(_ocenter), radius(_radius), color(_color), mintime(min_time),
  maxtime(max_time) {}

bool DynSphere::hit(const Ray& r, float tmin, float tmax, float time,
        HitRecord& record) const
{
    Vector3 new_center = getCenter(time);
    Vector3 temp = r.origin() - new_center;

    double a = dot( r.direction(), r.direction() );
    double b = 2*dot( r.direction(), temp );
    double c = dot( temp, temp ) - radius*radius;

    double discriminant = b*b- 4*a*c;

    // first check to see if ray intersects sphere
    if ( discriminant > 0 )
    {
        discriminant = sqrt( discriminant );
        double t = (- b - discriminant) / (2*a);
```

```cpp
        // now check for valid interval
        if (t < tmin)
            t = (- b + discriminant) / (2*a);
        if (t < tmin || t > tmax)
            return false;

        // we have a valid hit
        record.t = t;
        record.normal = unitVector(r.origin() + t* r.direction()
    - new_center);
        record.color  = color;
        return true;
    }
    return false;
}

bool DynSphere::shadowHit(const Ray& r, float tmin, float tmax,
        float time) const
{
    Vector3 new_center = getCenter(time);
    Vector3 temp = r.origin() - new_center;

    double a = dot( r.direction(), r.direction() );
    double b = 2*dot( r.direction(), temp );
    double c = dot( temp, temp ) - radius*radius;

    double discriminant = b*b- 4*a*c;

    // first check to see if ray intersects sphere
    if ( discriminant > 0 )
    {
        discriminant = sqrt( discriminant );
        double t = (- b - discriminant) / (2*a);

        // now check for valid interval
        if (t < tmin)
            t = (- b + discriminant) / (2*a);
        if (t < tmin || t > tmax)
            return false;

        // we have a valid hit
        return true;
    }
    return false;
}
```

```
Vector3 DynSphere::getCenter(float time)const
{
   float realtime = time * maxtime  + (1.0f - time) * mintime;
   return Vector3(ocenter.x() + realtime,
                  ocenter.y() + realtime,
                  ocenter.z() + realtime);
}
```

4.7 NOTES

A circular lens will give you a slightly more realistic camera model. The only obstacle to adding a circular lens is finding a method to sample the unit circle. The easiest solution is to sample a square and map these samples to a disk, so $\phi = 2\pi r_1$ and $r = R\sqrt{r_2}$, where (r, ϕ) is the polar coordinate on the disk, and R is the radius of the disk. Shirley and Chiu give the details of a more complicated but perhaps better mapping in "A Low Distortion Map Between Disk and Square" (*Journal of Graphics Tools*, 1997).

5 | Solid Texture Mapping

To make our images more realistic, we need to give the objects material properties, and we need to give the environment lighting. For now, we will assume objects are *matte*, i.e., that they are not shiny. To do this, we will give objects each a color $R(\mathbf{p})$ that can vary with position $\mathbf{p}$. For example, the colors of a magazine cover vary over position and can be described by a function R. Your ray tracer should just return $R(\mathbf{p})$ when it intersects an object at point $\mathbf{p}$. For many solid-colored objects, $R(\mathbf{p})$ is just a constant. But for objects with *texture*, we should expect $R(\mathbf{p})$ to vary as $\mathbf{p}$ moves across a surface. One way to do this is to create a *solid texture* that defines an RGB at every point in 3D space. When a ray hits a surface at $\mathbf{p}$, this function can be evaluated and the return value can be used for $R(\mathbf{p})$. Such a strategy is clearly suitable for surfaces that are "carved" from a solid medium, such as a marble sculpture. In this chapter, we describe how to add interesting solid textures to your system. More traditional surface textures are covered in the next chapter. Note that for software engineering reasons we consider solid-color objects just to be a simple case of texture, so we think of all objects as textured.

5.1 STRIPE TEXTURES

There are surprisingly many ways to make a striped texture. Let's assume we have two colors c_0 and c_1 that we want to make the stripe color. We need some oscillating function to switch between the two colors. An easy one is a cosine:

```
RGB stripe( Vector3 p )
if sin(p_z) > 0 then
    return c_0
else
    return c_1
```

Figure 5.1. Various stripe textures.

We can also make the stripe's width w controllable:

RGB stripe(Vector3 **p**, float w)
if $\sin(\pi p_z/w) > 0$ **then**
    return c_0
else
    return c_1

If we want to interpolate smoothly between the stripe colors we can use a parameter t:

RGB stripe(Vector3 **p**, float w)
float $t = (1 + \sin(\pi * p_z/w))/2$
return $t * c_0 + (1 - t) * c_1$

These three possibilities are shown in Figure 5.1.

    While we can make many procedural textures such as the stripe, typically we'd like to add some irregularity to textures. For example, while wood grain has an underlying stripe pattern, the stripes "wobble" in a semi-random manner. Such irregularity is a key to realism. Ideally, we'd like to take a procedural pattern and "warp" it as shown in Figure 5.2. Unfortunately, such warping is not easy to do procedurally, especially in a ray tracer where we would have to warp each point **p** independently at time of intersection. One way we might approach this is to set up a warping function $\mathbf{q}(\mathbf{p})$ that encodes the warping and passes **q** to the procedural texture. However, most procedural textures depend only on a scalar, so this is overkill. Instead, we can encode a slowly varying random number $n(\mathbf{p})$ through all of space. In our stripe texture, we can replace $\sin(p_x)$ with $\sin(p_x + n(\mathbf{p}))$. This will shift the peaks of the sine wave by an amount that varies with **p** because $n(\mathbf{p})$ varies. If we make sure n varies irregularly and continuously, we will in effect warp the function as desired. If n can be deterministically evaluated, then it will work for a ray tracer. We discuss the most popular way to implement n in the next section.

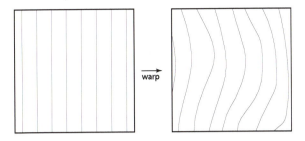

Figure 5.2. Irregularity could be added to a pattern by warping space. In practice this is too expensive.

5.2   SOLID NOISE

To design n, just calling a random number for every point wouldn't be appropriate because it would just be like "white noise" in TV static. We would like to make it smoother without losing the random quality. One possibility would be to blur white noise, but there is no practical implementation of this that can be evaluated in isolation. Another possibility would be to make a big lattice with a stored random number at every Cartesian lattice point (x, y, and z all integers) and interpolate these random points for points between lattice nodes. This would make the lattice too obvious, and you would need too much memory. Perlin introduced a modification of this basic idea that both hides the lattice and requires little memory. His function $n(\mathbf{p})$ is usually called *Perlin noise* and can be seen in a huge number of graphics images, and for which he received a technical Oscar.

Perlin used a variety of tricks to improve this basic lattice technique. First, he placed randomly-chosen vectors at the lattice points and used dot products to move the extrema off the lattice. Second, he used higher-order interpolation rather than trilinear to hide derivative artifacts. Finally, he used hashing so that he could use a small table for all the lattice points. Here is his basic method:

$$n(x, y, z) = \sum_{i=\lfloor x \rfloor}^{\lfloor x \rfloor + 1} \sum_{j=\lfloor y \rfloor}^{\lfloor y \rfloor + 1} \sum_{k=\lfloor z \rfloor}^{\lfloor z \rfloor + 1} \Omega_{ijk}(x - i, y - j, z - k)$$

where (x, y, z) are the Cartesian coordinates of $\mathbf{x}$, and

$$\Omega_{ijk}(u, v, w) = \omega(u)\omega(v)\omega(w)\left(\mathbf{g}_{ijk} \cdot (u, v, w)\right),$$

and $\omega(t)$ is the cubic weighting function:

$$\omega(t) = \begin{cases} -6|t|^6 + 15|t|^4 - 10|t|^3 + 1 & \text{if } |t| < 1, \\ 0 & \text{otherwise.} \end{cases}$$

The final piece is that g_{ijk} is a vector for the lattice point $(x, y, z) = (i, j, k)$. Since we want any potential ijk, we use a pseudorandom table:

$$g_{ijk} = \mathbf{G}\left(\phi(i + \phi(j + \phi(k)))\right)$$

where $\mathbf{G}$ is a precomputed array of N vectors, and $\phi(i) = P[i \mod N]$ where P is an array of length N containing a permutation of the integers 0 through $N - 1$. In practice, Perlin suggests $N = 16$ and the following vectors:

$$
\begin{aligned}
(\ 1,\ \ 1,\ \ 0) \\
(-1,\ \ 1,\ \ 0) \\
(\ 1, -1,\ \ 0) \\
(-1, -1,\ \ 0)
\end{aligned}
$$

$$
\begin{aligned}
(\ 1,\ \ 0,\ \ 1) \\
(-1,\ \ 0,\ \ 1) \\
(\ 1,\ \ 0, -1) \\
(-1,\ \ 0, -1)
\end{aligned}
$$

$$
\begin{aligned}
(\ 0,\ \ 1,\ \ 1) \\
(\ 0, -1,\ \ 1) \\
(\ 0,\ \ 1, -1) \\
(\ 0, -1, -1)
\end{aligned}
$$

$$
\begin{aligned}
(\ 1,\ \ 1,\ \ 0) \\
(-1,\ \ 1,\ \ 0) \\
(\ 0, -1,\ \ 1) \\
(\ 0, -1, -1).
\end{aligned}
$$

The first twelve vectors are from the origin to the twelve edges of a cube, and the next four are padding so that mod can be made efficient.

Because solid noise can be positive or negative, it must be transformed before being converted to a color. The absolute value of noise over a 10×10 square is shown in Figure 5.3 along with stretched versions. These versions are stretched by scaling the points input to the noise function.

The dark curves are where the original noise function went from positive to negative. Since noise varies from -1 to 1, a smoother image can be achieved by

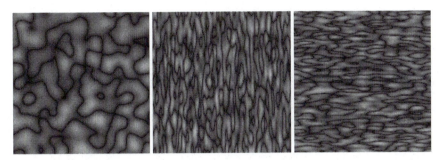

Figure 5.3. Absolute value of solid noise and noise for scaled x and y values.

using $(n(\mathbf{p}) + 1)/2$ for color. However, since noise values close to 1 or -1 are rare, this will be a fairly smooth image. Larger scaling can increase the contrast (Figure 5.4).

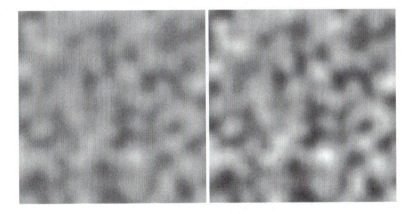

Figure 5.4. Using $0.5 * \text{noise} + 0.5$ (left) and $0.8 * \text{noise} + 0.5$ (right) for color.

5.3 TURBULENCE

Many natural textures contain a variety of feature sizes in the same texture. Perlin uses a pseudofractal "turbulence" function:

$$n_t(\mathbf{p}) = \sum_i^M \frac{n(2^i \mathbf{p})}{2^i}$$

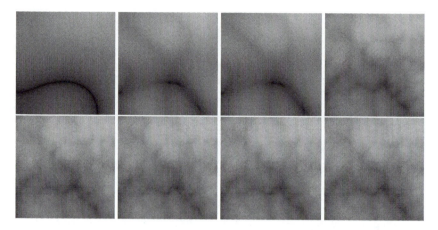

Figure 5.5. Turbulence function with one through eight terms in the summation.

The turbulence function is shown for various values of M in Figure 6.5. This can be used to distort the stripe function:

RGB turbstripe(Vector3 **p**, float w)
float $t = (1 + \sin(k_1 p_x + turbulence(k_2\mathbf{p})))/w)/2$
return $tc_0 + (1 - t)c_1$

Various values for k_1 and k_2 were used to generate Figure 5.6.

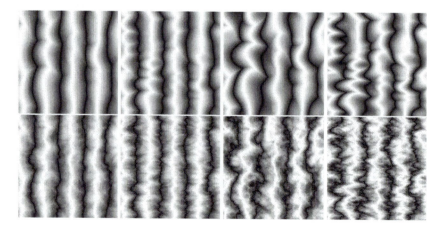

Figure 5.6. Various turbulent stripe textures with different k_1, k_2. The top row has only the first term of the turbulence series.

5.4 C++ CODE

5.4.1 Solid Noise Class

This code is extremely useful in many graphics applications. Some example uses
are procedural modeling, procedural texturing, and bump mapping.

```cpp
// SolidNoise.h

#ifndef _SOLID_NOISE_H_
#define _SOLID_NOISE_H_ 1

#include <math.h>
#include "Vector3.h"

class SolidNoise {
public:
    SolidNoise();
    float noise(const Vector3&) const;
    float turbulence(const Vector3& p, int depth) const;
    float dturbulence(const Vector3& p, int depth, float d) const;
    float omega(float t) const;
    Vector3 gamma(int i, int j, int k) const;
    int intGamma(int i, int j) const;
    float knot(int i, int j, int k, Vector3& v) const;

    Vector3 grad[16];
    int phi[16];
};

inline float SolidNoise::omega(float t) const {
    t = (t > 0.0f)? t : -t;
    // we can assume t is in [-1, 1] in this code so no extra 'if'
    needed return (-6.0f*t*t*t*t*t + 15.0f*t*t*t*t -10.0f*t*t*t + 1.0f);
}

inline Vector3 SolidNoise::gamma(int i, int j, int k) const
{
    int idx;
    idx = phi[abs(k)%16];
    idx = phi[abs(j + idx) % 16];
    idx = phi[abs(i + idx) % 16];
    return grad[idx];
}

inline float SolidNoise::knot(int i, int j, int k, Vector3& v)
```

```
   const { return (omega(v.x()) * omega(v.y()) * omega(v.z())
          * (dot(gamma(i,j,k),v)));
}

inline int SolidNoise::intGamma(int i, int j) const {
   int idx;
   idx = phi[abs(j)%16];
   idx = phi[abs(i + idx) % 16];
   return idx;
}

#endif // _SOLID_NOISE_H_


// SolidNoise.cc

#include "SolidNoise.h"
#include "RNG.h"

SolidNoise::SolidNoise()
{
   RNG random;
   int i;

   grad[0] = Vector3( 1, 1, 0);
   grad[1] = Vector3(-1, 1, 0);
   grad[2] = Vector3( 1,-1, 0);
   grad[3] = Vector3(-1,-1, 0);

   grad[4] = Vector3( 1, 0, 1);
   grad[5] = Vector3(-1, 0, 1);
   grad[6] = Vector3( 1, 0,-1);
   grad[7] = Vector3(-1, 0,-1);

   grad[8] = Vector3( 0, 1, 1);
   grad[9] = Vector3( 0,-1, 1);
   grad[10]= Vector3( 0, 1,-1);
   grad[11]= Vector3( 0,-1,-1);

   grad[12]= Vector3( 1, 1, 0);
   grad[13]= Vector3(-1, 1, 0);
   grad[14]= Vector3( 0,-1, 1);
   grad[15]= Vector3( 0,-1,-1);

   for (i = 0; i < 16; i++)
      phi[i] = i;
```

```
    // shuffle phi
    for (i = 14; i >= 0; i--) {
        int target = int(random()*i);
        int temp = phi[i+1];
        phi[i+1] = phi[target];
        phi[target] = temp;
    }
}


float SolidNoise::turbulence(const Vector3& p, int depth)
const
{
    float sum = 0.0f;
    float weight = 1.0f;
    Vector3 ptemp(p);

    sum = fabs(noise(ptemp));

    for (int i = 1; i < depth; i++)
    {
        weight = weight * 2;
        ptemp.setX(p.x() * weight);
        ptemp.setY(p.y() * weight);
        ptemp.setZ(p.z() * weight);

        sum += fabs(noise(ptemp)) / weight;
    }
    return sum;
}

float SolidNoise::dturbulence(const Vector3& p, int depth, float d)
const {
    float sum = 0.0f;
    float weight = 1.0f;
    Vector3 ptemp(p);

    sum += fabs(noise(ptemp)) / d;

    for (int i = 1; i < depth; i++)
    {
        weight = weight * d;
        ptemp.setX(p.x() * weight);
        ptemp.setY(p.y() * weight);
        ptemp.setZ(p.z() * weight);
```

```
        sum += fabs(noise(ptemp)) / d;
    }
    return sum;
}

float SolidNoise::noise(const Vector3& p) const {
    int fi, fj, fk;
    float fu, fv, fw, sum;
    Vector3 v;

    fi = int(floor(p.x()));
    fj = int(floor(p.y()));
    fk = int(floor(p.z()));
    fu = p.x() - float(fi);
    fv = p.y() - float(fj);
    fw = p.z() - float(fk);
    sum = 0.0;

    v = Vector3(fu, fv, fw);
    sum += knot(fi, fj, fk, v);

    v = Vector3(fu - 1, fv, fw);
    sum += knot(fi + 1, fj, fk, v);

    v = Vector3(fu, fv - 1, fw);
    sum += knot(fi, fj + 1, fk, v);

    v = Vector3(fu, fv, fw -1);
    sum += knot(fi, fj, fk + 1, v);

    v = Vector3(fu -1, fv -1, fw);
    sum += knot(fi + 1, fj + 1, fk, v);

    v = Vector3(fu -1, fv, fw -1);
    sum += knot(fi + 1, fj, fk + 1, v);

    v = Vector3(fu, fv -1, fw -1);
    sum += knot(fi, fj + 1, fk + 1, v);

    v = Vector3(fu -1, fv -1, fw -1);
    sum += knot(fi + 1, fj + 1, fk + 1, v);

    return sum;
}
```

5.4.2 Texture Class

There is a question of how to store information about the object's material and color attributes. We could store the data with each primitive but this is very memory expensive, especially considering that you will usually have many primitives that share the same material type (e.g., a triangle mesh model). We recommend using a virtual *texture* class for storing the color attributes for primitives. Now each primitive need only store a pointer to a texture (or material).

Below we give a sample implementation of a texture class and a few solid texture types. Simple solid textures such as checkers and fuzzy stripes are straightforward to add. With a little ingenuity, the noise class can be used to create more complex textures such as realistic wood.

One implementational question that arises is where to calculate the color of the intersected point on the hit object. We could have the object calculate its color within the *hit* function and then pass it back in the hit record as we have done before. However, the color calculation is now a potentially costly procedure and we should probably delay the evaluation until we have found the nearest intersected shape in the ray's path. For this and other reasons that will arise later, we recommend passing back a pointer to the texture of the hit shape and letting the renderer directly query the texture object.

We will change the HitRecord structure as follows:

```
struct HitRecord
{
    float t;
    Vector3 normal;
    Vector2 uv;          // we will use this for 2D textures
    Vector3 hit_p;       // the point of intersection
    Texture* hit_tex;    // the nearest intersected object's texture
};
```

We pass two parameters into the virtual *value* function. The *Vector3* parameter is the 3D hit point we are shading (hit_p in the hit record). The *Vector2* parameter will be used in the next chapter to implement 2D texture maps.

```
// Texture.h

#ifndef _TEXTURE_H_
#define _TEXTURE_H_ 1

#include "Vector2.h"
#include "Vector3.h"
#include "rgb.h"

class Texture
```

```
{
public:
   // The Vector2 is a UV coord and the Vector3 is the 3D hit point
   virtual rgb value(const Vector2&, const Vector3&) const = 0;
};


#endif // _TEXTURE_H_
```

5.4.3   Noise Texture Class

This class will not only help in debugging the somewhat complex noise algorithm, but also yields interesting pictures.

```
// NoiseTexture.h

#ifndef _NOISE_TEXTURE_H_
#define _NOISE_TEXTURE_H_ 1

#include <math.h>
#include "Texture.h"
#include "rgb.h"
#include "SolidNoise.h"

class NoiseTexture : public Texture
{
public:
   NoiseTexture(float _scale = 1.0f)
   {
      scale = _scale;
      c0 = rgb(0.8,0.0,0.0);
      c1 = rgb(0.0,0.0,0.8);
   }

   NoiseTexture(const rgb & _c0, const rgb & _c1, float _scale = 1.0f)
      : c0(_c0), c1(_c1), scale(_scale) {}

   virtual rgb value(const Vector2& uv, const Vector3& p) const;

   float scale;
   rgb c0, c1;
   SolidNoise solid_noise;
};


#endif // _NOISE_TEXTURE_H_

// NoiseTexture.cc
```

```
#include "NoiseTexture.h"

rgb NoiseTexture::value(const Vector2& uv, const Vector3& p) const
{
   float t = (1.0f + solid_noise.noise(p * scale)) / 2.0f  ;
   return t*c0 + (1.0f - t)*c1;
}
```

5.4.4   Simple Texture Class

This class is used for constant color objects.

```
// SimpleTexture.h

#ifndef _SIMPLE_TEXTURE_H_
#define _SIMPLE_TEXTURE_H_

#include "Texture.h"

class SimpleTexture : public Texture
{
public:
   SimpleTexture(rgb c) { color = c;}
   virtual rgb value(const Vector2&, const Vector3&) const
   { return color; }

   rgb color;
};


#endif // _SIMPLE_TEXTURE_H_
```

5.4.5   Marble Texture Class

This class creates wonderful images but requires some parameter tweaking to make things look right.

```
// MarbleTexture.h

#ifndef _MARBLE_TEXTURE_H_
#define _MARBLE_TEXTURE_H_ 1

#include <math.h>
#include "Texture.h"
```

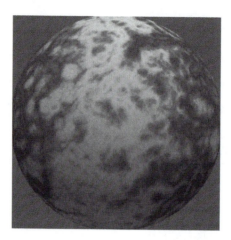

Figure 5.7. A sphere created with our MarbleTexture class. The sphere has a center at the origin and a radius of 10. The marble texture has *stripes per area* of .15 and a *scale* of 5.

```cpp
#include "rgb.h"
#include "SolidNoise.h"

class MarbleTexture : public Texture
{
public:
   MarbleTexture(float stripes_per_unit, float _scale = 5.0f,
int _octaves = 8)
   {
      freq = M_PI * stripes_per_unit;
      scale = _scale;
      octaves = _octaves;
      c0 = rgb(0.8,0.8,0.8);
      c1 = rgb(0.4,0.2,0.1);
      c2 = rgb(0.06, 0.04,0.02);
   }
      MarbleTexture(const rgb & _c0, const rgb & _c1, const rgb & _c2,
         float stripes_per_unit, float _scale = 3.0f,
   int _octaves = 8)
      : c0(_c0), c1(_c1), c2(_c2)
   {
      freq = M_PI * stripes_per_unit;
      scale = _scale;
      octaves = _octaves;
   }

   virtual rgb value(const Vector2& uv, const Vector3& p) const;
```

```
    float freq, scale;
    int octaves;
    rgb c0, c1, c2;
    SolidNoise noise;
};


#endif // _MARBLE_TEXTURE_H_


// MarbleTexture.cc

#include "MarbleTexture.h"

rgb MarbleTexture::value(const Vector2& uv, const Vector3& p) const
{
    float temp = scale*noise.turbulence(freq*p, octaves);
    float t = 2.0f*fabs(sin(freq*p.x() + temp));

    if (t < 1.0f)
        return (c1*t + (1.0f - t)*c2);
    else
    {
        t -= 1.0f;
        return (c0*t + (1.0f - t)*c1);
    }
}
```

5.5 NOTES

Ken Perlin introduced the noise function in 1984. The version given in this chapter is from "Hypertexture" (Perlin and Hoffert, *Computer Graphics (Proc. SIGGRAPH '89)*, 1989) and "Improving Noise" (Perlin, *Transactions on Computer Graphics (Proc. SIGGRAPH '02)*, 2002). A discussion of how to design procedural solid textures can be found in *Texturing & Modeling: A Procedural Approach* (Ebert et al. 3rd edition, Morgan Kaufmann, 2002), and *The Renderman Companion: A Programmer's Guide to Realistic Computer Graphics* (Upstill, Addison-Wesley, 1990).

6 | Image Texture Mapping

We often want to take a pixel-based image and "map" it onto a surface. This is not difficult to implement once you understand the coordinate systems involved. In the last chapter, we used the point on a surface to look up a texture. Here, we use a 2D coordinate, often called uv, which is used to create a reflectance $R(u, v)$.

The key is to take an image and associate a (u, v) coordinate system on it so that it can be associated with points on a 3D surface. For example, if the latitudes and longitudes on the world map are associated with polar coordinate systems on the sphere, we get a globe (Figure 6.1).

As is true in Figure 6.1, it is crucial that the coordinates on the image and the object match in "just the right way." As a convention, the coordinate system on the image is set to be the unit square $(u, v) \in [0, 1] \times [0, 1]$. For (u, v) outside of this square, only the fractional parts of the coordinates are used, resulting in a tiling of the plane (Figure 6.2). Note that the image has a different number of pixels horizontally and vertically so the image pixels have a nonuniform aspect ratio in (u, v) space. To map this $(u, v) \in [0, 1] \times [0, 1]$ image onto a sphere, we

Figure 6.1. A cylindrical projection world map and its placement on the sphere. The distortions in the texture map (i.e., Greenland being so large) exactly correspond to the shrinking that occurs when the map is applied to the sphere.

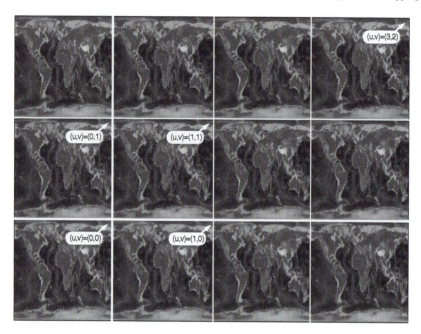

Figure 6.2. The tiling of an image onto the (u, v) plane. Note that the input image is rectangular and that this rectangle is mapped to a unit square on the (u, v) plane.

first compute the spherical coordinates. (Recall the coordinate system shown in Figure 6.3). For a sphere of radius R and with center (c_x, c_y, c_z), the parametric equation of the sphere is

$$
\begin{aligned}
x &= x_c + R \cos \phi \sin \theta, \\
y &= y_c + R \sin \phi \sin \theta, \\
z &= z_c + R \cos \theta.
\end{aligned}
$$

The (θ, ϕ) can be found using

$$
\begin{aligned}
\theta &= \arccos \frac{z - z_c}{R}, \\
\phi &= \arctan2(y - y_c, x - x_c),
\end{aligned}
$$

where $\arctan2(a, b)$ is the *atan2* of most math libraries which returns the arctangent of a/b. Because $(\theta, \phi) \in [0, \pi] \times [-\pi, \pi]$, we convert to (u, v) as follows,

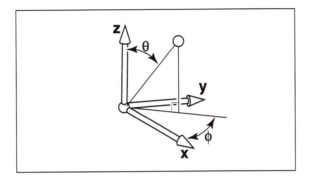

Figure 6.3. Spherical coordinates.

after first adding 2π to ϕ if it is negative:

$$u = \frac{\phi}{2\pi},$$
$$v = \frac{\pi - \theta}{\pi}.$$

This mapping is shown in Figure 6.4. There is a similar, although typically more complicated, way to generate coordinates for most 3D shapes.

Once the (u, v) coordinate of an object is known, all that remains is to find the corresponding color in the image. First, we remove the integer portion of (u, v) so that it is in the unit square. We then use one of three interpolation strategies to compute the image color for that coordinate. The simplest strategy is to treat

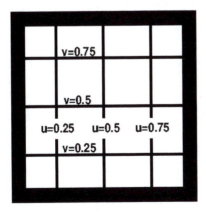
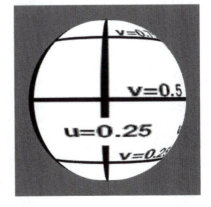

Figure 6.4. Left: A calibration texture map, useful for debugging. Right: The sphere viewed along the y axis.

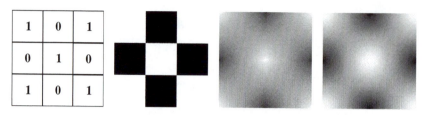

Figure 6.5. Right to left: Values in texture file, point texture, bilinear texture, and bicubic texture.

each image pixel as a constant-colored rectangular tile. This is shown on the left of Figure 6.5. To compute this, apply $c(u, v) = c_{ij}$, where $c(u, v)$ is the texture color at (u, v) and c_{ij} is the pixel color for pixel indices

$$
\begin{aligned}
i &= \lfloor un_x \rfloor \\
j &= \lfloor vn_y \rfloor,
\end{aligned}
$$

where (n_x, n_y) is the size of the image being textured, and the indices start at $(i, j) = (0, 0)$.

For a smoother texture, a bilinear interpolation can be used as shown in the middle of Figure 6.5. Here we use the formula

$$
\begin{aligned}
c(u, v) = \; &(1 - u')(1 - v')c_{ij} + \\
&u'(1 - v')c_{(i+1)j} + \\
&(1 - u')v'c_{i(j+1)} + \\
&u'v'c_{(i+1)(j+1)},
\end{aligned}
$$

where $(u', v') = (nu - \lfloor nu \rfloor, nv - \lfloor nv \rfloor)$. The discontinuities in the derivative in intensity can cause visible mach bands, so hermite smoothing can be used:

$$
\begin{aligned}
c(u, v) = \; &(1 - u'')(1 - v'')c_{ij} + \\
&u''(1 - v'')c_{(i+1)j} + \\
&(1 - u'')v''c_{i(j+1)} + \\
&u''v''c_{(i+1)(j+1)}
\end{aligned}
$$

where $(u'', v'') = (3(u')^2 - 2(u')^3, 3(v')^2 - 2(v')^3)$, which results in the rightmost image of Figure 6.5.

6.1 C++ CODE

We give code for the image texture class and a sphere primitive that supports texture coordinates. To add a *UVTriangle* class, you simply store *UV* coordinates along with each vertex of the triangle. You can then use barycentric interpolation to determine the *UV* value at an arbitrary hit point on the triangle.

6.1.1   2D Texture Class

```
// ImageTexture.h

#ifndef _IMAGE_TEXTURE_H_
#define _IMAGE_TEXTURE_H_

#include "Texture.h"

class Image;

class ImageTexture : public Texture
{
public:
   ImageTexture(char* file_name);
   virtual rgb value(const Vector2& uv, const Vector3& p) const;

   Image* image;
};
#endif // _IMAGE_TEXTURE_H_


// ImageTexture.cc

#include <ImageTexture.h>
#include <Image.h>

ImageTexture::ImageTexture(char* filename)
{
   image = new Image();
   image->readPPM(filename);
}

rgb ImageTexture::value(const Vector2& uv, const Vector3& p) const
{
   float u = uv.x() - int(uv.x());
   float v = uv.y() - int(uv.y());
   u *= (image->width()-3);
   v *= (image->height()-3);

   int iu = (int)u;
   int iv = (int)v;

   float tu = u-iu;
   float tv = v-iv;

   rgb c = image->getPixel(iu,iv)*(1-tu)*(1-tv)+
      image->getPixel(iu+1,iv)*tu*(1-tv)+
      image->getPixel(iu,iv+1)*(1-tu)*tv+
      image->getPixel(iu+1,iv+1)*tu*tv;

   return c;
}
```

6.1.2   UVSphere Class

This class implements a sphere with a vertical axis parallel to the z axis. In order to have an arbitrary vertical axis, you can add a *Vector3* data member that determines the up direction for the sphere.

```
// UVSphere.h

#ifndef _UV_SPHERE_H_
#define _UV_SPHERE_H_ 1

#include "Shape.h"
#include "Vector3.h"
#include "Ray.h"
#include "Texture.h"

class UVSphere : public Shape
{
public:
    UVSphere(const Vector3& _center, float _radius, Texture* tex);
    BBox boundingBox() const;
    bool hit(const Ray& r, float tmin, float tmax, float time,
 HitRecord& record) const;
    bool shadowHit(const Ray& r, float tmin, float tmax, float time) const;

    Vector3 center;
    float radius;
    Texture* tex;
};

#endif // _UV_SPHERE_H__


// UVSphere.cc

#include "UVSphere.h"

UVSphere::UVSphere(const Vector3& _center, float _radius, Texture* _tex)
    : center(_center), radius(_radius), tex(_tex) {}


bool UVSphere::hit(const Ray& r, float tmin, float tmax, float time,
     HitRecord* record)const
{
    Vector3 temp = r.origin() - center;

    double a = dot( r.direction(), r.direction() );
    double b = 2*dot( r.direction(), temp );
    double c = dot( temp, temp ) - radius*radius;

    double discriminant = b*b- 4.0*a*c;
```

```
   // first check to see if ray intersects sphere
   if ( discriminant > 0.0 )
   {
      discriminant = sqrt( discriminant );
      double t = (- b - discriminant) / (2.0*a);

      // now check for valid interval
      if (t < tmin)
         t = (- b + discriminant) / (2.0*a);
      if (t < tmin || t > tmax)
         return false;

      // we have a valid hit
      rec.t = t;
      rec.hit_p = (r.origin() + t* r.direction());
      Vector3 n = record.normal = (rec.hit_p - center) / radius;

      // calculate UV coordinates
      float twopi = 6.28318530718f;
      float theta = acos( n.z());
      float phi   = atan2(n.y(), n.x());
      if (phi < 0.0f) phi += twopi;

      float one_over_2pi = .159154943092f;
      float one_over_pi  = .318309886184f;
      rec.uv = Vector2(phi*one_over_2pi, (M_PI - theta) * one_over_pi);

      record.hit_tex = tex;
      return true;
   }
   return false;
}

bool UVSphere::shadowHit(const Ray& r, float tmin, float tmax,
      float time)const
{
   Vector3 temp = r.origin() - center;

   double a = dot( r.direction(), r.direction() );
   double b = 2*dot( r.direction(), temp );
   double c = dot( temp, temp ) - radius*radius;

   double discriminant = b*b- 4*a*c;

   // first check to see if ray intersects sphere
   if ( discriminant > 0 )
   {
      discriminant = sqrt( discriminant );
      double t = (- b - discriminant) / (2*a);

      // now check for valid interval
      if (t < tmin)
         t = (- b + discriminant) / (2*a);
```

```
    if (t < tmin || t > tmax)
        return false;

    // we have a valid hit
    return true;
  }
  return false;
}
```

6.2 NOTES

A nice overview of texture mapping is "A Survey of Texture Mapping (Heckbert, *IEEE Computer Graphics*, 1986). You might want to allow images to be used for the background in your program. A good overview of such *environment mapping* is available in the tutorials section of www.nvidia.com under the keyword *cubemap*.

7 | Triangle Meshes

Most real-world models are composed of complexes of triangles with shared vertices. In many fields, these are known as *triangular meshes* or *triangular irregular networks* (TINs). In this chapter, we describe how to manage these types of models without too much storage.

A simple triangular mesh is shown in Figure 7.1. You could store these three triangles as independent entities and thus store point p_1 three times, and the other vertices twice each for a total of nine stored points (three vertices for each of two triangles). In addition, you are storing a pointer to a texture object for each individual triangle. As an alternative, you could try to somehow share the common vertices and store only four vertices and one texture pointer. So instead of

class triangle
texture* t
Vector3 $p_0, p_1, p_2,$

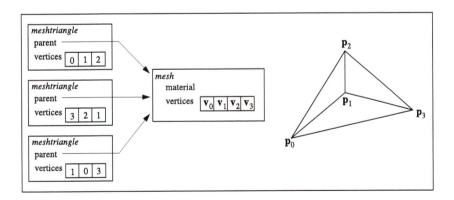

Figure 7.1. A three triangle mesh with four vertices v_i, each containing a location p_i possibly with other vertex data.

you would have two classes:

  class mesh
  texture* t
  array of Vector3 vertices

and

  class meshtriangle
  pointer to mesh meshptr
  int i_0, i_1, i_2,

where i_0, i_1, and i_2 are indices into the *vertices* array. Either the triangle class or the mesh class will work. Is there a space advantage for the mesh class? Typically, a large mesh has each vertex being stored by about six triangles, although there can be any number for extreme cases. This means about two triangles for each shared vertex. If you have n triangles, then there are about $n/2$ vertices in the shared case and $3n$ in the unshared case, but when you share, you get an extra $3n$ integers and n pointers. Since you don't have to store the texture in each mesh triangle, that saves n pointers, which cancels out the storage for *meshptr*. If we assume that the data for floats, pointers, and integers all take the same storage (a dubious assumption), the triangles will take $10n$ storage units and the mesh will take $5.5n$ storage units. So this amounts to around a factor of two, which has generally been true for the real implementations we have seen. Is this factor of two worth the complication? We think the answer is yes as soon as you start adding "properties" to the vertices.

Each vertex can have material parameters, texture coordinates, irradiances, and essentially any parameter that a renderer might use. In practice, these parameters are bilinearly interpolated across the triangle. So, if a triangle is intersected at barycentric coordinates (β, γ), you interpolate the (u, v) coordinates the same way you interplate points. Recall that the point at the barycentric coordinate (β, γ) is

$$\mathbf{p}(\beta, \gamma) = \mathbf{p}_0 + \beta(\mathbf{p}_1 - \mathbf{p}_0) + \gamma(\mathbf{p}_2 - \mathbf{p}_0).$$

A similar equation applies for (u, v):

$$
\begin{aligned}
u(\beta, \gamma) &= u_0 + \beta(u_1 - u_0) + \gamma(u_2 - u_0), \\
v(\beta, \gamma) &= v_0 + \beta(v_1 - v_0) + \gamma(v_2 - v_0).
\end{aligned}
$$

$$(7.1)$$

Several ways in which a texture could be applied by changing the (u, v) at triangle vertices are shown in Figure 7.2.

Another common type of vertex data stored is a *normal*. We can then interpolate the normal in much the same way as we did (u, v) coordinates to achieve smooth, rather than faceted, shading. This type of shading, in which we interpolate the normal, is known is *Phong shading*.

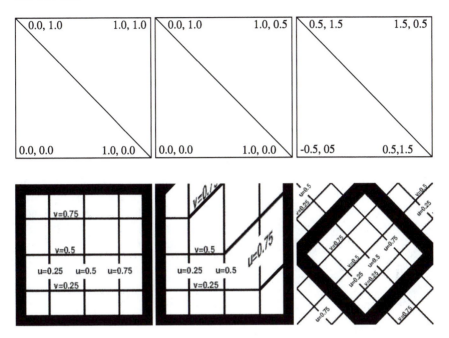

Figure 7.2. Various mesh textures obtained by changing (u, v) coordinates stored at vertices.

7.1 C++ CODE

7.1.1 Vertex Classes

```cpp
// Vertex.h

#ifndef _VERTEX_H_
#define _VERTEX_H_ 1

#include "Vector2.h"
#include "Vector3.h"

struct VertexUV
{
   Vector3 vertex;
   Vector2 uv;
};

struct VertexN
{
   Vector3 vertex;
   Vector3 normal;
};
```

```
struct VertexUVN
{
    Vector3 vertex;
    Vector3 normal;
    Vector2 uv;
};

#endif // _VERTEX_H_
```

7.1.2   Mesh Class

This simple mesh class can be used with any of the three types of vertices or
with 3D vectors. One drawback is that the mesh can only contain one texture. In
order to support models made of several textures, you will need to either break
the model up into several meshes or store a texture index with each MeshTriangle
in order to index into an array of textures stored with the mesh.

```
// Mesh.h

#ifndef _MESH_H_
#define _MESH_H_ 1

#include "Vertex.h"
#include "Shape.h"
#include "Texture.h"


class Mesh
{
public:
    Mesh() {}
    ~Mesh() {}
    Texture* getTexture()const { return tex; }

    // data members
    Texture*    tex;
    Vector3*    verts;
    VertexUV*   vertUVs;
    VertexN*    vertNs;
    VertexUVN*  vertUVNs;
};

#endif // _MESH_H_
```

7.1.3   Mesh Triangle

We have given a sample implementation of a mesh triangle class that supports
(u, v) coordinates. It is straightforward to add classes that support different vertex
properties.

```
// MeshTriangle.h

#ifndef _MESH_TRI_H_
#define _MESH_TRI_H_ 1

#include "Shape.h"

class Mesh;
class Texture;

class MeshTriangleUV : public Shape
{
public:
   MeshTriangleUV();
   MeshTriangleUV(Mesh* _Mesh, int p0, int p1, int p2, int index);
   ~MeshTriangleUV();
   bool hit(const Ray& r, float tmin, float tmax, float time,
         HitRecord& rec)const;
   bool shadowHit(const Ray& r, float tmin, float tmax, float time)const;

   // data members
   int p[3];
   Mesh* mesh_ptr;
};

#endif // _MESH_TRI_H_



// MeshTriangle.h

#include "Mesh.h"
#include "MeshTriangle.h"



MeshTriangleUV::MeshTriangleUV(){}

MeshTriangleUV::MeshTriangleUV(Mesh* _Mesh, int p0, int p1, int p2, int index)
   : mesh_ptr(_Mesh)
{ p[0] = p0; p[1] = p1; p[2] = p2; }

MeshTriangleUV::~MeshTriangleUV(){}

bool
MeshTriangleUV::hit(const Ray& r, float tmin, float tmax,
      float time, HitRecord& rec)const
{
   Vector3 p0((mesh_ptr->vertUVs[p[0]]).vertex);
   Vector3 p1((mesh_ptr->vertUVs[p[1]]).vertex);
   Vector3 p2((mesh_ptr->vertUVs[p[2]]).vertex);

   float tval;
```

```
float A = p0.x() - p1.x();
float B = p0.y() - p1.y();
float C = p0.z() - p1.z();

float D = p0.x() - p2.x();
float E = p0.y() - p2.y();
float F = p0.z() - p2.z();

float G = r.direction().x();
float H = r.direction().y();
float I = r.direction().z();

float J = p0.x() - r.origin().x();
float K = p0.y() - r.origin().y();
float L = p0.z() - r.origin().z();

float EIHF = E*I-H*F;
float GFDI = G*F-D*I;
float DHEG = D*H-E*G;

float denom = (A*EIHF + B*GFDI + C*DHEG);

float beta = (J*EIHF + K*GFDI + L*DHEG) / denom;

if (beta <= 0.0f || beta >= 1.0f) return false;

float AKJB = A*K - J*B;
float JCAL = J*C - A*L;
float BLKC = B*L - K*C;

float gamma = (I*AKJB + H*JCAL + G*BLKC)/denom;
if (gamma <= 0.0f || beta + gamma >= 1.0f) return false;

tval =  -(F*AKJB + E*JCAL + D*BLKC) / denom;
if (tval >= tmin && tval <= tmax)
{
    // if prim is hit, fill hit_rec
    double alpha = 1.0 - beta - gamma;
    Vector2 u0((mesh_ptr->vertUVs[p[0]]).uv);
    Vector2 u1((mesh_ptr->vertUVs[p[1]]).uv);
    Vector2 u2((mesh_ptr->vertUVs[p[2]]).uv);
    rec.uv = Vector2(alpha*u0.x() + beta*u1.x() + gamma*u2.x(),
        alpha*u0.y() + beta*u1.y() + gamma*u2.y());

    rec.texture = mesh_ptr->getTexture();
    rec.t = tval;
    rec.normal = unitVector(cross((p1 - p0), (p2 - p0)));

    return true;
}
return false;
}
```

```cpp
bool
MeshTriangleUV::shadowHit(const Ray& r, float tmin, float tmax,
                 float time)const
{
   Vector3 p0((mesh_ptr->vertUVs[p[0]]).vertex);
   Vector3 p1((mesh_ptr->vertUVs[p[1]]).vertex);
   Vector3 p2((mesh_ptr->vertUVs[p[2]]).vertex);

   float tval;
   float A = p0.x() - p1.x();
   float B = p0.y() - p1.y();
   float C = p0.z() - p1.z();

   float D = p0.x() - p2.x();
   float E = p0.y() - p2.y();
   float F = p0.z() - p2.z();

   float G = r.direction().x();
   float H = r.direction().y();
   float I = r.direction().z();

   float J = p0.x() - r.origin().x();
   float K = p0.y() - r.origin().y();
   float L = p0.z() - r.origin().z();

   float EIHF = E*I-H*F;
   float GFDI = G*F-D*I;
   float DHEG = D*H-E*G;

   float denom = (A*EIHF + B*GFDI + C*DHEG);

   float beta = (J*EIHF + K*GFDI + L*DHEG) / denom;

   if (beta <= 0.0f || beta >= 1.0f) return false;

   float AKJB = A*K - J*B;
   float JCAL = J*C - A*L;
   float BLKC = B*L - K*C;

   float gamma = (I*AKJB + H*JCAL + G*BLKC)/denom;
   if (gamma <= 0.0f || beta + gamma >= 1.0f) return false;

   tval =  -(F*AKJB + E*JCAL + D*BLKC) / denom;

   return (tval >= tmin && tval <= tmax);
}
```

7.2 NOTES

Managing huge meshes (and procedural models in general) is discussed in "Rendering Complex Scenes with Memory-Coherent Ray Tracing" (Pharr et al., *Proceedings of SIGGRAPH '97, Computer Graphics Proceedings, Annual Conference Series*, 1997). There are many alternate implementations to the one presented in this chapter (e.g., the MeshTriangles can store pointers directly to the vertices), and only testing determines which is most efficient on a given architecture.

8 | Instancing

This chapter discusses *instancing*, where an object is stored in its own local coordinates along with a separate transform matrix. In a conventional z-buffer graphics system, each vertex of the object is transformed by the matrix before being drawn. So if a scale in z by 0.5 is applied, the object will become squat in that dimension. In ray tracing, instancing is easy to manage, but the way the transforms are done is a little trickier to understand than with a z-buffer, as you will see. The basic idea of instancing for ray tracing is shown in Figure 8.1. A neat thing about instancing is that you can have the same object be associated with two different "instances" which have different values for the transform.

A wonderful thing about instances is that although they require only a few lines of code, you can create more primitives. For example, if you implement a sphere, you can get ellipsoids by having scaled instances.

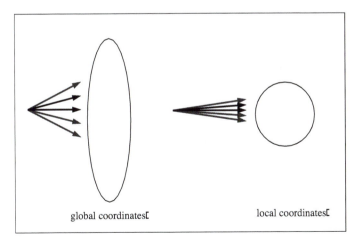

global coordinates

local coordinates

Figure 8.1. If rays and objects are all transformed together, the image remains the same. This can change the problem of ray tracing ellipsoids into the easier problem of intersecting with a sphere.

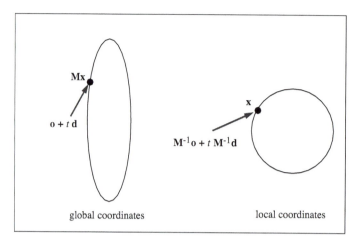

Figure 8.2. A ray traced against an ellipsoid can be transformed so that the ellipsoid becomes a sphere centered at the origin.

8.1 TRANSFORMATION MATRICES

You should implement a class *transform-matrix* which stores a 4×4 matrix of scalars. So a matrix has values

$$\mathbf{M} = \begin{bmatrix} m_{00} & m_{01} & m_{02} & m_{03} \\ m_{10} & m_{11} & m_{12} & m_{13} \\ m_{20} & m_{21} & m_{22} & m_{23} \\ 0 & 0 & 0 & 1 \end{bmatrix}.$$

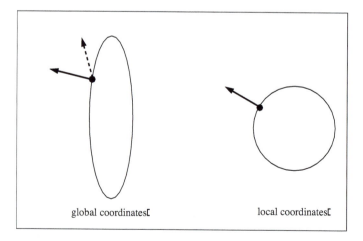

Figure 8.3. When the normal vector in local coordinates is transformed as a conventional vector, you get a non-normal vector (dotted). A different transformation rule is needed for normals to get the solid vector.

This matrix is used to transform vectors to other vectors. For convenience, we advocate storing the inverse matrix $\mathbf{N} = \mathbf{M}^{-1}$ along with $\mathbf{M}$. You can also, of course, not bother to store the bottom row of the matrix. Note that the matrix should transform points and displacements and normal vectors differently. We will not go over the details of why these matrices work the way they do here; for more information, see any introductory computer graphics book.

Suppose we are given a transform matrix $\mathbf{M}$ and a point (location) $\mathbf{p}$; then, the transform rule is

$$\mathbf{Mp} = \begin{bmatrix} m_{00} & m_{01} & m_{02} & m_{03} \\ m_{10} & m_{11} & m_{12} & m_{13} \\ m_{20} & m_{21} & m_{22} & m_{23} \\ m_{30} & m_{31} & m_{32} & m_{33} \end{bmatrix} \begin{bmatrix} p_x \\ p_y \\ p_z \\ 1 \end{bmatrix} = \begin{bmatrix} m_{00}p_x + m_{01}p_y + m_{02}p_z + m_{03} \\ m_{10}p_x + m_{11}p_y + m_{12}p_z + m_{13} \\ m_{20}p_x + m_{21}p_y + m_{22}p_z + m_{23} \\ m_{30}p_x + m_{31}p_y + m_{32}p_z + m_{33} \end{bmatrix}.$$

In practice, all the matrices we deal with will have a bottom row of $(0, 0, 0, 1)$, so the transformed point will have a one for its last coordinate.

Because vectors indicate a direction, they do not change when translated (e.g., "North" is the same everywhere). But we do want to have scales and rotate count. Fortunately, we can use the row that points set to one to manage this for the transform of a vector $\mathbf{v}$:

$$\mathbf{Mv} = \begin{bmatrix} m_{00} & m_{01} & m_{02} & m_{03} \\ m_{10} & m_{11} & m_{12} & m_{13} \\ m_{20} & m_{21} & m_{22} & m_{23} \\ m_{30} & m_{31} & m_{32} & m_{33} \end{bmatrix} \begin{bmatrix} v_x \\ v_y \\ v_z \\ 0 \end{bmatrix} = \begin{bmatrix} m_{00}v_x + m_{01}v_y + m_{02}v_z \\ m_{10}v_x + m_{11}v_y + m_{12}v_z \\ m_{20}v_x + m_{21}v_y + m_{22}v_z \\ m_{30}v_x + m_{31}v_y + m_{32}v_z \end{bmatrix}.$$

So when we transform a ray $\mathbf{p}(t) = \mathbf{o} + t\mathbf{v}$, we need to make sure we transform $\mathbf{o}$ and $\mathbf{v}$ according to location and displacement rules, respectively. In your code, this implies that you should have separate functions such as "transformAsLocation," "transformAsOffset," and "transformAsNormal."

Surface normal vectors transform a different way still (Figure 8.4). Instead of $\mathbf{Mn}$, as it would be for a conventional vector, it is $(\mathbf{M}^{-1})^T\mathbf{n}$, where T indicates transpose. If you follow our recommendation and store $\mathbf{N} = \mathbf{M}^{-1}$, this gives

$$(\mathbf{M}^{-1})^T\mathbf{n} = \mathbf{N}^T\mathbf{n} \begin{bmatrix} n_{00} & n_{10} & n_{20} & n_{30} \\ n_{01} & n_{11} & n_{21} & n_{31} \\ n_{02} & n_{12} & n_{22} & n_{32} \\ n_{03} & n_{13} & n_{23} & n_{33} \end{bmatrix} \begin{bmatrix} v_x \\ v_y \\ v_z \\ 0 \end{bmatrix} = \begin{bmatrix} n_{00}v_x + n_{10}v_y + n_{20}v_z \\ n_{01}v_x + n_{11}v_y + n_{21}v_z \\ n_{02}v_x + n_{12}v_y + n_{22}v_z \\ n_{03}v_x + n_{13}v_y + n_{23}v_z \end{bmatrix}.$$

The first operator the matrix should have is *transform-location*, which takes the location $\mathbf{o}$ to anothor location $\mathbf{o}'$:

$$\begin{bmatrix} o'_x \\ o'_y \\ o'_z \\ 1 \end{bmatrix} = \begin{bmatrix} m_{00} & m_{01} & m_{02} & m_{03} \\ m_{10} & m_{11} & m_{12} & m_{13} \\ m_{20} & m_{21} & m_{22} & m_{23} \\ 0 & 0 & 0 & 1 \end{bmatrix} \begin{bmatrix} o_x \\ o_y \\ o_z \\ 1 \end{bmatrix} = \begin{bmatrix} m_{00}o_x + m_{01}o_y + m_{02}o_z + m_{03} \\ m_{10}o_x + m_{11}o_y + m_{12}o_z + m_{13} \\ m_{20}o_x + m_{21}o_y + m_{22}o_z + m_{23} \\ 1 \end{bmatrix}.$$

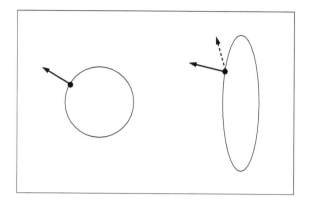

Figure 8.4. When the normal vector in local coordinates is transformed as a conventional vector, you get a non-normal vector (dotted). A different transformation rule is needed for normals to get the solid (not dotted) vector.

This matrix is used to transfer vectors to other vectors. Since vectors do not get changed when translated, we "turn off" the last column of the matrix for a vector **v**:

$$\begin{bmatrix} v'_x \\ v'_y \\ v'_z \\ 0 \end{bmatrix} = \begin{bmatrix} m_{00} & m_{01} & m_{02} & m_{03} \\ m_{10} & m_{11} & m_{12} & m_{13} \\ m_{20} & m_{21} & m_{22} & m_{23} \\ 0 & 0 & 0 & 1 \end{bmatrix} \begin{bmatrix} v_x \\ v_y \\ v_z \\ 0 \end{bmatrix} = \begin{bmatrix} m_{00}v_x + m_{01}v_y + m_{02}v_z \\ m_{10}v_x + m_{11}v_y + m_{12}v_z \\ m_{20}v_x + m_{21}v_y + m_{22}v_z \\ 0 \end{bmatrix}.$$

The surface normal vector $\mathbf{n}'$ to a surface transformed by $\mathbf{M}$ is

$$\mathbf{n}' = \left(\mathbf{M}^{-1}\right)^T \mathbf{n} = \begin{bmatrix} n_{00} & n_{11} & n_{20} & 0 \\ n_{01} & n_{11} & n_{21} & 0 \\ n_{02} & n_{12} & n_{22} & 0 \\ n_{03} & n_{13} & n_{23} & 1 \end{bmatrix} \mathbf{n},$$

where n_{ij} are the elements of $\mathbf{N} = \mathbf{M}^{-1}$.

Your class should contain both $\mathbf{M}$ and $\mathbf{N}$, and should have functions to transform points, vectors, and surface normal vectors. This is a total of six functions: three for each of two matrices.

You will also need functions or constructors for common matrix types—the first is an identity that leaves points unchanged:

$$\text{Identity} = \begin{bmatrix} 1 & 0 & 0 & 0 \\ 0 & 1 & 0 & 0 \\ 0 & 0 & 1 & 0 \\ 0 & 0 & 0 & 1 \end{bmatrix}.$$

To translate (move), by a vector $\mathbf{t} = (t_x, t_y, t_z)$:

$$\text{translate}(\mathbf{t}) = \begin{bmatrix} 1 & 0 & 0 & t_x \\ 0 & 1 & 0 & t_y \\ 0 & 0 & 1 & t_z \\ 0 & 0 & 0 & 1 \end{bmatrix}.$$

To scale by coefficients (s_x, s_y, s_z):

$$\text{scale}(s_x, s_y, s_z) = \begin{bmatrix} s_x & 0 & 0 & 0 \\ 0 & s_y & 0 & 0 \\ 0 & 0 & s_z & 0 \\ 0 & 0 & 0 & 1 \end{bmatrix}.$$

To rotate counterclockwise around the x, y, or z axis by angle θ:

$$\text{rotate-x}(\theta) = \begin{bmatrix} 1 & 0 & 0 & 0 \\ 0 & \cos\theta & -\sin\theta & 0 \\ 0 & \sin\theta & \cos\theta & 0 \\ 0 & 0 & 0 & 1 \end{bmatrix},$$

$$\text{rotate-y}(\theta) = \begin{bmatrix} \cos\theta & 0 & \sin\theta & 0 \\ 0 & 1 & 0 & 0 \\ -\sin\theta & 0 & \cos\theta & 0 \\ 0 & 0 & 0 & 1 \end{bmatrix},$$

$$\text{rotate-z}(\theta) = \begin{bmatrix} \cos\theta & -\sin\theta & 0 & 0 \\ \sin\theta & \cos\theta & 0 & 0 \\ 0 & 0 & 1 & 0 \\ 0 & 0 & 0 & 1 \end{bmatrix}.$$

For more arbitrary rotations, we employ ONBs. This may be the most important measure to avoid ugly programs, so make sure you absorb this part of the material if you aren't familiar with it.

Suppose we want to find the unique rotation matrix which takes the ONB defined by $\mathbf{u}$, $\mathbf{v}$, $\mathbf{w}$ to the canonical ONB defined by $\mathbf{x}$, $\mathbf{y}$, $\mathbf{z}$ (Figure 8.5). A nice way to work out what matrix is required to represent that transform. Whatever this matrix is, its inverse will take the canonical basis in the other direction, i.e., it will take $\mathbf{x}$ to $\mathbf{u}$, $\mathbf{y}$ to $\mathbf{v}$, and $\mathbf{z}$ to $\mathbf{w}$. So if we assume $\mathbf{Mx} = \mathbf{u}$, we can see what the first column of the matrix is. The following matrix accomplishes exactly that:

$$\begin{bmatrix} u_x & & & 0 \\ u_y & & & 0 \\ u_z & & & 0 \\ 0 & 0 & 0 & 1 \end{bmatrix} \begin{bmatrix} 1 \\ 0 \\ 0 \\ 0 \end{bmatrix} = \begin{bmatrix} u_x \\ u_y \\ u_z \\ 0 \end{bmatrix}.$$

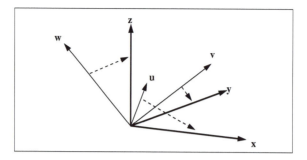

Figure 8.5. Some rotation matrix takes an ONB defined by **u**, **v**, **w** to the canonical ONB defined by **x**, **y**, **z**.

You can verify that there are no other possibilities for these numbers in the first column, and that the numbers in the blank fields don't matter. We can observe similar behavior by transforming the **y** and **z** axes to determine

$$\text{rotate-xyz-to-uvw} = \begin{bmatrix} u_x & v_x & w_x & 0 \\ u_y & v_y & w_y & 0 \\ u_z & v_z & w_z & 0 \\ 0 & 0 & 0 & 1 \end{bmatrix}.$$

Because the algebraic inverse of a transform matrix is always the matrix that performs the opposite geometric transform, and the algebraic inverse of a rotation matrix is its transpose, we know

$$\text{rotate-uvw-to-xyz} = \begin{bmatrix} u_x & u_y & u_z & 0 \\ v_x & v_y & v_z & 0 \\ w_x & w_y & w_z & 0 \\ 0 & 0 & 0 & 1 \end{bmatrix}.$$

This transpose property assumes the matrix is orthonormal, which all rotation matrices are. If we apply this matrix to **u** we get

$$\begin{bmatrix} u_x & u_y & u_z & 0 \\ v_x & v_y & v_z & 0 \\ w_x & w_y & w_z & 0 \\ 0 & 0 & 0 & 1 \end{bmatrix} \begin{bmatrix} u_x \\ u_y \\ u_z \\ 0 \end{bmatrix} = \begin{bmatrix} \mathbf{u} \cdot \mathbf{u} \\ \mathbf{v} \cdot \mathbf{u} \\ \mathbf{w} \cdot \mathbf{u} \\ 0 \end{bmatrix} = \begin{bmatrix} 1 \\ 0 \\ 0 \\ 0 \end{bmatrix}.$$

The dot products $\mathbf{v} \cdot \mathbf{u}$ and $\mathbf{w} \cdot \mathbf{u}$ are zero because **u**, **v**, and **w** are mutually orthogonal. Similiar behavior is true for transforming **v** and **w**.

8.1.1   Using Transformation Matrices

Transform matrices are usually applied in series. So, for example, to rotate a sphere centered at **c** about its own center by an angle θ, where the "north pole" is an axis in direction **a**, we

1. move the sphere to the origin ($\mathbf{M}_1$),

2. rotate **a** to align with **z** ($\mathbf{M}_2$),

3. rotate by θ about **z** ($\mathbf{M}_3$),

4. rotate **z** back to **a** ($\mathbf{M}_2^{-1}$),

5. move the sphere back to **c** ($\mathbf{M}_1^{-1}$).

Algebraically, this composite transform **M** is given by

$$\mathbf{M} = \mathbf{M}_1^{-1}\mathbf{M}_2^{-1}\mathbf{M}_3\mathbf{M}_2\mathbf{M}_1.$$

Because the vector is multiplied on the right of the matrix, the transforms that are applied first are on the right. , matrix is $\mathbf{M}_2$ which aligns **a** with **z**. This is surprisingly easy: Just construct an ONB where **w** is aligned to **a** as described earlier, and then create a *rotate-uvw-to-xyz* matrix as described earlier.

8.2   INTERSECTING RAYS WITH TRANSFORMED OBJECTS

The basic idea of how to do intersections with transformed objects is shown in Figure 8.2. Rather than transforming the points on the object, which might be complicated, we transform the ray. We use the convention that the "local" points on the object are transformed by **M**. This means the *opposite* transform should bring the ray *into* local coordinates. This transformed ray, $\mathbf{M}^{-1}\mathbf{o}+t\mathbf{M}^{-1}\mathbf{d}$, is intersected with the object in its native local coordinate system and the intersection point is **x**.

The intersection point in *world* coordinates is **Mx**. If the local normal vector is **n**, then the transformed normal that we use for lighting computations is $(\mathbf{M}^{-1})^T\mathbf{x}$.

An interesting issue is whether we implement solid textures with local or glocal coordinates. Usually, using local coordinates is the right answer, so that the texture will move with the object as the object is changed.

One implication of instancing is that the length of the vector in rays cannot be restricted to one. We need arbitrary vector lengths so that they can be scaled into the local coordinate system; if **d** had length one, a scaled version of **d** in local coordinates could have any length.

The pseudocode for the intersection with a surface *surf* transformed by a matrix **M** is given below:

function hit-instance(ray $\mathbf{o} + t\mathbf{d}$)
$\mathbf{o}' \leftarrow (\mathbf{M}^{-1})\mathbf{o}$
$\mathbf{d}' \leftarrow (\mathbf{M}^{-1})\mathbf{d}$ {if hit-surf returns true, assume hit point **p**' and normal **n**' are somehow returned}
if hit-surf($\mathbf{o}' + t\mathbf{d}'$) **then**
   $\mathbf{p} \leftarrow \mathbf{M}\mathbf{p}'$
   $\mathbf{n} \leftarrow (\mathbf{M}^{-1})^T\mathbf{n}'$
   return true
else
   return false

8.3   LATTICES

Instances can be used to create procedural complexity without code that is specific to a specific type of geometric object. This is accomplished by making many copies of the same object with different transform matrices. This essentially makes copies of objects. A procedural way to make this is with a "lattice" that creates a 3D array of object copies. If we have a way to create a transformed instance *create-instance(surf,*M*)*, the pseudocode for a lattice is as follows:

for all $i \in \{0, \ldots n_x\}, j \in \{0, \ldots n_y\}, k \in \{0, \ldots n_y\}$ **do**
   $\mathbf{M} \leftarrow$ translate(ax + i*dx, ay + j*dy, az + k*dz) {(ax,ay,az) is the startpoint and (dx,dy,dz) is the base offset}
   create-instance(object,M)

8.4   C++ CODE

8.4.1   Matrix Library

Note that the inversion functions given in this class assume that the matrix is nonsingular.

```
// Matrix.h

#ifndef _MATRIX_H_
#define _MATRIX_H_ 1

#include "Vector3.h"
#include "iostream.h"
```

```cpp
#include "iomanip.h"
#include "math.h"

class Matrix
{
public:
   Matrix() {}
   Matrix(const Matrix & orig);

   void invert();
   void transpose();
   Matrix getInverse()const;
   Matrix getTranspose()const;

   Matrix & operator+= (const Matrix& right_op);
   Matrix & operator-= (const Matrix& right_op);
   Matrix & operator*= (const Matrix& right_op);
   Matrix & operator*= (float right_op);

   friend Matrix operator- (const Matrix& left_op, const Matrix& right_op);
   friend Matrix operator+ (const Matrix& left_op, const Matrix& right_op);
   friend Matrix operator* (const Matrix& left_op, const Matrix& right_op);
   friend Vector3 operator* (const Matrix& left_op, const Vector3& right_op);
   friend Matrix operator* (const Matrix & left_op, float right_op);

   friend Vector3 transformLoc(const Matrix& left_op, const Vector3& right_op);
   friend Vector3 transformVec(const Matrix& left_op, const Vector3& right_op);

   friend Matrix zeroMatrix();
   friend Matrix identityMatrix();
   friend Matrix translate(float _x, float _y, float _z);
   friend Matrix scale(float _x, float _y, float _z);
   friend Matrix rotate(const Vector3 & axis, float angle);
   friend Matrix rotateX(float angle);     //
   friend Matrix rotateY(float angle);     // More efficient than arbitrary axis
   friend Matrix rotateZ(float angle);     //
   friend Matrix viewMatrix(const Vector3& eye, const Vector3 & gaze,
         const Vector3& up);
   friend ostream & operator<< (ostream& out, const Matrix& right_op);

   float determinant();
   float x[4][4];
};

// 3x3 matrix determinant -- helper function
inline float det3 (float a, float b, float c,
                   float d, float e, float f,
                   float g, float h, float i)
{ return a*e*i + d*h*c + g*b*f - g*e*c - d*b*i - a*h*f; }

#endif    // _MATRIX_H_
```

```
// Matrix.cc

#include "Matrix.h"

Matrix::Matrix (const Matrix & right_op)
{
   for (int i = 0; i < 4; i++)
     for (int j = 0; j < 4; j++)
        x[i][j] = right_op.x[i][j];
}


Matrix& Matrix::operator+= (const Matrix & right_op)
{
   for (int i = 0; i < 4; i++)
     for (int j = 0; j < 4; j++)
        x[i][j] += right_op.x[i][j];
   return *this;
}


Matrix& Matrix::operator-= (const Matrix & right_op)
{
   for (int i = 0; i < 4; i++)
     for (int j = 0; j < 4; j++)
        x[i][j] -= right_op.x[i][j];
   return *this;
}


Matrix& Matrix::operator*= (float right_op)
{
   for (int i = 0; i < 4; i++)
     for (int j = 0; j < 4; j++)
        x[i][j] *= right_op;
   return *this;
}


Matrix& Matrix::operator*= (const Matrix & right_op)
{
   Matrix ret = *this;

   for (int i = 0; i < 4; i++)
     for (int j = 0; j < 4; j++)
       {
 float sum = 0;
 for (int k = 0; k < 4; k++)
   sum += ret.x[i][k] * right_op.x[k][j];
 x[i][j] = sum;
       }
   return *this;
}


void Matrix::invert()
{
   float det = determinant();
```

```
Matrix inverse;
inverse.x[0][0]  = det3(x[1][1], x[1][2], x[1][3],
                        x[2][1], x[2][2], x[2][3],
                        x[3][1], x[3][2], x[3][3]) / det;
inverse.x[0][1] = -det3(x[0][1], x[0][2], x[0][3],
                        x[2][1], x[2][2], x[2][3],
                        x[3][1], x[3][2], x[3][3]) / det;
inverse.x[0][2]  = det3(x[0][1], x[0][2], x[0][3],
                        x[1][1], x[1][2], x[1][3],
                        x[3][1], x[3][2], x[3][3]) / det;
inverse.x[0][3] = -det3(x[0][1], x[0][2], x[0][3],
                        x[1][1], x[1][2], x[1][3],
                        x[2][1], x[2][2], x[2][3]) / det;

inverse.x[1][0] = -det3(x[1][0], x[1][2], x[1][3],
                        x[2][0], x[2][2], x[2][3],
                        x[3][0], x[3][2], x[3][3]) / det;
inverse.x[1][1]  = det3(x[0][0], x[0][2], x[0][3],
                        x[2][0], x[2][2], x[2][3],
                        x[3][0], x[3][2], x[3][3]) / det;
inverse.x[1][2] = -det3(x[0][0], x[0][2], x[0][3],
                        x[1][0], x[1][2], x[1][3],
                        x[3][0], x[3][2], x[3][3]) / det;
inverse.x[1][3]  = det3(x[0][0], x[0][2], x[0][3],
                        x[1][0], x[1][2], x[1][3],
                        x[2][0], x[2][2], x[2][3]) / det;

inverse.x[2][0]  = det3(x[1][0], x[1][1], x[1][3],
                        x[2][0], x[2][1], x[2][3],
                        x[3][0], x[3][1], x[3][3]) / det;
inverse.x[2][1] = -det3(x[0][0], x[0][1], x[0][3],
                        x[2][0], x[2][1], x[2][3],
                        x[3][0], x[3][1], x[3][3]) / det;
inverse.x[2][2]  = det3(x[0][0], x[0][1], x[0][3],
                        x[1][0], x[1][1], x[1][3],
                        x[3][0], x[3][1], x[3][3]) / det;
inverse.x[2][3] = -det3(x[0][0], x[0][1], x[0][3],
                        x[1][0], x[1][1], x[1][3],
                        x[2][0], x[2][1], x[2][3]) / det;


inverse.x[3][0] = -det3(x[1][0], x[1][1], x[1][2],
                        x[2][0], x[2][1], x[2][2],
                        x[3][0], x[3][1], x[3][2]) / det;
inverse.x[3][1]  =  det3(x[0][0], x[0][1], x[0][2],
                        x[2][0], x[2][1], x[2][2],
                        x[3][0], x[3][1], x[3][2]) / det;
inverse.x[3][2] = -det3(x[0][0], x[0][1], x[0][2],
                        x[1][0], x[1][1], x[1][2],
                        x[3][0], x[3][1], x[3][2]) / det;
inverse.x[3][3]  =  det3(x[0][0], x[0][1], x[0][2],
                        x[1][0], x[1][1], x[1][2],
                        x[2][0], x[2][1], x[2][2]) / det;
```

```
      *this = inverse;
}

Matrix Matrix::getInverse()const
{
   Matrix ret = *this;
   ret.invert();
   return ret;
}

void Matrix::transpose()
{
   for (int i = 0; i < 4; i++)
      for (int j = 0; j < 4; j++)
      {
 float temp = x[i][j];
 x[i][j] = x[j][i];
 x[j][i] = temp;
      }
}

Matrix Matrix::getTranspose()const
{
   Matrix ret = *this;
   ret.transpose();

   return ret;
}

Vector3 transformLoc(const Matrix& left_op, const Vector3& right_op)
{ return left_op * right_op; }

Vector3 transformVec(const Matrix& left_op, const Vector3& right_op)
{
   Vector3 ret;

   ret[0] = right_op[0] * left_op.x[0][0] + right_op[1] * left_op.x[0][1] +
            right_op[2] * left_op.x[0][2];
   ret[1] = right_op[0] * left_op.x[1][0] + right_op[1] * left_op.x[1][1] +
            right_op[2] * left_op.x[1][2];
   ret[2] = right_op[0] * left_op.x[2][0] + right_op[1] * left_op.x[2][1] +
            right_op[2] * left_op.x[2][2];

   return ret;

}

Matrix zeroMatrix ()
{
   Matrix ret;
   for (int i = 0; i < 4; i++)
      for (int j = 0; j < 4; j++)
         ret.x[i][j] = 0.0;
```

```
      return ret;
  }

  Matrix identityMatrix()
  {
      Matrix ret;
      ret.x[0][0] = 1.0;
      ret.x[0][1] = 0.0;
      ret.x[0][2] = 0.0;
      ret.x[0][3] = 0.0;
      ret.x[1][0] = 0.0;
      ret.x[1][1] = 1.0;
      ret.x[1][2] = 0.0;
      ret.x[1][3] = 0.0;
      ret.x[2][0] = 0.0;
      ret.x[2][1] = 0.0;
      ret.x[2][2] = 1.0;
      ret.x[2][3] = 0.0;
      ret.x[3][0] = 0.0;
      ret.x[3][1] = 0.0;
      ret.x[3][2] = 0.0;
      ret.x[3][3] = 1.0;
      return ret;
  }

  Matrix translate (float _x, float _y, float _z)
  {
      Matrix ret = identityMatrix();

      ret.x[0][3] = _x;
      ret.x[1][3] = _y;
      ret.x[2][3] = _z;

      return ret;
  }

  // angle is in radians
  Matrix rotateX (float angle)
  {
      Matrix ret = identityMatrix();

      float cosine = cos(angle);
      float sine   = sin(angle);

      ret.x[1][1] = cosine;
      ret.x[1][2] =  -sine;
      ret.x[2][1] =   sine;
      ret.x[2][2] = cosine;

      return ret;
  }

  // angle is in radians
```

```
Matrix rotateY (float angle)
{
   Matrix ret = identityMatrix();

   float cosine = cos(angle);
   float sine   = sin(angle);

   ret.x[0][0] = cosine;
   ret.x[0][2] =   sine;
   ret.x[2][0] =  -sine;
   ret.x[2][2] = cosine;

   return ret;
}

// angle is in radians
Matrix rotateZ (float angle)
{
   Matrix ret = identityMatrix();

   float cosine = cos(angle);
   float sine   = sin(angle);

   ret.x[0][0] = cosine;
   ret.x[0][1] =  -sine;
   ret.x[1][0] =   sine;
   ret.x[1][1] = cosine;

   return ret;
}

// rotation is in radians about an arbitrary axis
Matrix
rotate(const Vector3 & axis, float angle)
{
   Vector3 _axis = unitVector(axis);
   Matrix ret;
   float x = _axis.x();
   float y = _axis.y();
   float z = _axis.z();
   float cosine = cos(angle);
   float sine = sin(angle);
   float t   = 1 - cosine;

   ret.x[0][0] = t * x * x + cosine;
   ret.x[0][1] = t * x * y - sine * y;
   ret.x[0][2] = t * x * z + sine * y;
   ret.x[0][3] = 0.0;

   ret.x[1][0] = t * x * y + sine * z;
   ret.x[1][1] = t * y * y + cosine;
   ret.x[1][2] = t * y * z - sine * x;
   ret.x[1][3] = 0.0;
```

```
   ret.x[2][0] = t * x * z - sine * y;
   ret.x[2][1] = t * y * z + sine * x;
   ret.x[2][2] = t * z * z + cosine;
   ret.x[2][3] = 0.0;

   ret.x[3][0] = 0.0;
   ret.x[3][1] = 0.0;
   ret.x[3][2] = 0.0;
   ret.x[3][3] = 1.0;

   return ret;
}

Matrix scale(float _x, float _y, float _z)
{
   Matrix ret = zeroMatrix();

   ret.x[0][0] = _x;
   ret.x[1][1] = _y;
   ret.x[2][2] = _z;
   ret.x[3][3] = 1.0;

   return ret;
}

// creates viewing Matrix that so the ey is at xyz origin looking down the -z axis
Matrix
viewMatrix(const Vector3 & eye, const Vector3 & gaze, const Vector3 & up)
{
   Matrix ret = identityMatrix();

   // create an orthoganal basis from parameters
   Vector3 w = -(unitVector(gaze));
   Vector3 u = unitVector(cross(up, w));
   Vector3 v = cross(w, u);

   // rotate orthoganal basis to xyz basis
   ret.x[0][0] = u.x();
   ret.x[0][1] = u.y();
   ret.x[0][2] = u.z();
   ret.x[1][0] = v.x();
   ret.x[1][1] = v.y();
   ret.x[1][2] = v.z();
   ret.x[2][0] = w.x();
   ret.x[2][1] = w.y();
   ret.x[2][2] = w.z();

   // translare eye to xyz origin
   Matrix move = identityMatrix();
   move.x[0][3] = -(eye.x());
   move.x[1][3] = -(eye.y());
   move.x[2][3] = -(eye.z());
```

```
      ret = ret * move;
      return ret;
}

Matrix operator+ (const Matrix & left_op, const Matrix & right_op)
{
   Matrix ret;

   for (int i = 0; i < 4; i++)
      for (int j = 0; j < 4; j++)
 ret.x[i][j] = left_op.x[i][j] + right_op.x[i][j];

   return ret;
}

Matrix operator- (const Matrix & left_op, const Matrix & right_op)
{
   Matrix ret;

   for (int i = 0; i < 4; i++)
      for (int j = 0; j < 4; j++)
         ret.x[i][j] = left_op.x[i][j] - right_op.x[i][j];

   return ret;
}

Matrix operator* (const Matrix & left_op, float right_op)
{
   Matrix ret;

   for (int i = 0; i < 4; i++)
      for (int j = 0; j < 4; j++)
         ret.x[i][j] = left_op.x[i][j] * right_op;

   return ret;
}

Matrix operator* (const Matrix & left_op, const Matrix & right_op)
{
   Matrix ret;

   for (int i = 0; i < 4; i++)
      for (int j = 0; j < 4; j++)
         {
 float subt = 0.0;
 for (int k = 0; k < 4; k++)
    subt += left_op.x[i][k] * right_op.x[k][j];
 ret.x[i][j] = subt;
         }

   return ret;
}
```

```cpp
// transform a vector by matrix
Vector3 operator* (const Matrix & left_op, const Vector3 & right_op)
{
    Vector3 ret;
    float temp;

    ret[0] = right_op[0] * left_op.x[0][0] + right_op[1] * left_op.x[0][1] +
             right_op[2] * left_op.x[0][2] +           left_op.x[0][3];
    ret[1] = right_op[0] * left_op.x[1][0] + right_op[1] * left_op.x[1][1] +
             right_op[2] * left_op.x[1][2] +           left_op.x[1][3];
    ret[2] = right_op[0] * left_op.x[2][0] + right_op[1] * left_op.x[2][1] +
             right_op[2] * left_op.x[2][2] +           left_op.x[2][3];
    temp   = right_op[0] * left_op.x[3][0] + right_op[1] * left_op.x[3][1] +
             right_op[2] * left_op.x[3][2] +           left_op.x[3][3];

    ret /= temp;
    return ret;
}

ostream & operator<< (ostream & out, const Matrix & right_op)
{
    for (int i = 0; i < 4; i++)
    {
        for (int j = 0; j < 4; j++)
    out << setprecision(3) << setw(10) << right_op.x[i][j];
        out << endl;
    }
    return out;
}

float Matrix::determinant()
{
    float det;
    det  = x[0][0] * det3(x[1][1], x[1][2], x[1][3],
                          x[2][1], x[2][2], x[2][3],
                          x[3][1], x[3][2], x[3][3]);
    det -= x[0][1] * det3(x[1][0], x[1][2], x[1][3],
                          x[2][0], x[2][2], x[2][3],
                          x[3][0], x[3][2], x[3][3]);
    det += x[0][2] * det3(x[1][0], x[1][1], x[1][3],
                          x[2][0], x[2][1], x[2][3],
                          x[3][0], x[3][1], x[3][3]);
    det -= x[0][3] * det3(x[1][0], x[1][1], x[1][2],
                          x[2][0], x[2][1], x[2][2],
                          x[3][0], x[3][1], x[3][2]);
    return det;
}
```

8.4.2   Shape Instance Class

Here we give a simple Instancing class. You might want to create a time varying
instance class for use in animations and motion blurred images. To do this you
will simply have your transform be a function of time. The downside is that the
inverse needs to be computed for each hit.

```cpp
// Shape.h

#ifndef _INSTANCE_H_
#define _INSTANCE_H_ 1

#include "Shape.h"
#include "Matrix.h"

class Matrix;

class Instance : public Shape
{
public:
   Instance () {}
   ~Instance() {}
   Instance(Matrix trans, Matrix trans_inverse, Shape* _prim);
   Instance(Matrix trans, Shape* _prim);
   bool hit(const Ray& r, float tmin, float tmax, float time,
         HitRecord& rec)const;
   bool shadowHit(const Ray& r, float tmin, float tmax, float time)const;

   Matrix M;
   Matrix N;
   Shape* prim;
};

#endif // _INSTANCE_H_


// Instance.cc

#include "Instance.h"

Instance::Instance(Matrix trans, Matrix trans_inverse, Shape* _prim)
: M(trans), N(trans_inverse), prim(_prim) {}

Instance::Instance(Matrix trans, Shape* _prim)
: M(trans), N(trans) ,prim(_prim)
{ N.invert(); }

bool Instance::hit(const Ray& r, float tmin, float tmax, float time,
      HitRecord& rec)const
{
   Vector3 no = transformLoc(N, r.origin());
   Vector3 nd = transformVec(N, r.direction());
```

```
    Ray tray(no, nd);

    if (prim->hit(tray, tmin, tmax, time, rec))
    {
        rec.p = transformLoc(M, rec.p);
        Vector3 normal = transformVec(N.getTranspose(), rec.uvw.w());
        ONB uvw;
        uvw.initFromW(normal);
        rec.uvw = uvw;
        return true;
    }
    else return false;
}

bool Instance::shadowHit(const Ray& r, float tmin, float tmax, float time)const
{
    Vector3 no = transformLoc(N, r.origin());
    Vector3 nd = transformVec(N, r.direction());
    Ray tray(no, nd);

    return (prim->shadowHit(tray, tmin, tmax, time));
}
```

8.5 NOTES

A nice discussion of transforming normal vectors is available in the *OpenGL Programming Guide* (Woo et al., Addison-Wesley, 3rd Ed., 1999), which has a wonderful discussion of transformation matrices in general. Note that the intersection routine only requires one matrix without its inverse, so a clever implementation could reduce memory by avoiding storage of both the matrix and its inverse.

9 | Bounding Volume Hierarchies

This chapter describes how to use a bounding volume hierarchy (BVH) to avoid explicitly computing intersections with every object in the scene. This is similar to how binary search is used to speed searches in ordered 1D data. However, it is somewhat more complicated because ordering objects in 3D is somewhat ill-defined. There are many alternative acceleration strategies to the one presented here, and interested readers should consult the chapter notes. The BVH is our favorite because we believe it is the easiest to code and the most robust of current algorithms. Whether it is the fastest depends on the dataset, and which algorithm is usually fastest is an open question. In practice it does provide logarithmic searches, so it will provide huge speed increases over brute-force intersection tests for large models.

9.1 HIERARCHICAL BOUNDING BOXES

The basic idea of hierarchical bounding boxes can be seen by the common tactic of placing an axis-aligned 3D bounding box around all the objects as shown in Figure 9.1. Rays that hit the bounding box will actually be more expensive than in a brute force search because testing for intersection with the box is not free. However, rays that miss the box are cheaper than the brute force search. Such bounding boxes can be made hierarchical by partitioning the set of objects in a box and placing a box around each partition as shown in Figure 9.2.

The data structure for the hierarchy shown in Figure 9.3 might be a tree with the large bounding box at the root and the two smaller bounding boxes as left and right subtrees. These would, in turn, each point to a list of three triangles. The intersection of a ray with this particular hard-coded tree would be:

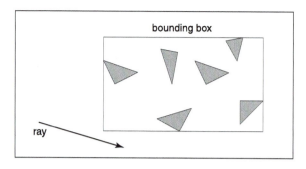

Figure 9.1. The ray is only tested for intersection with the surfaces if it hits the bounding box.

if (ray hits root box) **then**
    if (ray hits left subtree box) **then**
      check three triangles for intersection
    if (ray intersects right subtree box) **then**
      check other three triangles for intersection
    if (an intersections returned from each subtree) **then**
      return the closest of the two hits
    else if *(a intersection is returned from exactly one subtree)* **then**
      return that intersection
    else
      return false
else
    return false

Some observations related to this algorithm are that there is no geometric ordering between the two subtrees, and there is no reason a ray might not hit both subtrees. Indeed, there is no reason that the two subtrees might not overlap. A key point of

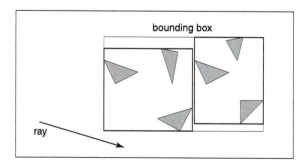

Figure 9.2. The bounding boxes can be nested by creating boxes around subsets of the model.

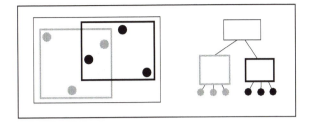

Figure 9.3. The grey box is a tree node that points to the three grey spheres, and the thick black box points to the three black spheres. Note that not all spheres enclosed by the box are guaranteed to be pointed to by the corresponding tree node.

such data hierarchies is that a box is guaranteed to bound all objects that are below it in the hierarchy, but they are *not* guaranteed to have all objects that overlap it spatially, as shown in Figure 9.3 This makes this geometric search somewhat more complicated than a traditional binary search on strictly ordered 1D data. The reader may note that several possible optimizations present themselves—we defer optimizations until we have a full hierarchical algorithm.

If we restrict the tree to be binary, and if each node in the tree has a bounding box, then this traversal code extends naturally. Further, assume that all nodes are either leaves in the tree and contain a primitive, or that they contain two subtrees/leaves. The *bvh-node* class should be of type Shape, so it should implement *Shape::hit*. The data it contains should be simple:

Shape* left
Shape* right
Box bbox.

The traversal code can then be called recursively in an object-oriented style.

Note that because *left* and *right* point to Shapes rather than BVH specifically, we can let the virtual functions take care of distinguishing between internal and leaf nodes; the appropriate *hit* function will be called for whatever is pointed to. Note that if the tree is built properly, we can eliminate the check for any of the pointers being *NULL*.

There are many ways to build a tree for a bounding volume hierarchy. It is convenient to make the tree binary, and roughly balanced, and to have the boxes of sibling subtrees not overlap too much. One common heuristic to accomplish this is to sort the surfaces along an axis before dividing them into two sublists. However, we have found it better to split evenly in space so the subtrees contain about the same amount of space rather than the same amount of objects. To do this we partition the list based on space:

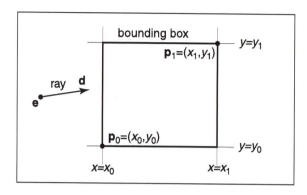

Figure 9.4. A 2D ray $e + t d$ is tested against a 2D bounding box defined by corners p_0 and p_1.

find the midpoint m of the bounding box of A along AXIS
partition A into lists with lengths k and (N-k) surrounding m
left = new node(A[0..k], (AXIS +1)   mod 3)
right = new node(A[k+1..N-1], (AXIS +1)   mod 3)
bbox = combine(left-node→ bbox, right-node→ bbox)

Although this results in an unbalanced tree, it allows for easy traversal of empty space and is cheaper to build because the partitioning is cheaper than sorting.

9.2   EFFICIENT RAY–BOX INTERSECTION

A key operation in BVH code is computing the intersection of a ray with an axis-aligned bounding box that encloses some objects (Figure 9.4). If the box is missed we need not test any of the objects it bounds. This differs from conventional ray-object intersection tests in that we do not need to know where the ray hits the box; we only need to know whether it hits the box.

The ray-box intersection code often ends up being the bottleneck, so it is important to write it very tightly as above. Note that *hitbox* is a member of *Box*. The *box* class is *not* a subclass of *Shape*. Its only job is to bound objects and return intersections. It does not have material properties, so it is never rendered directly. However, you may find it useful to also implement a *box-surface* as a distinct class that is renderable and implements *Shape::hit*.

To build up an algorithm for ray-box intersection, we begin by considering a 2D ray whose direction vector has positive x and y components. We can generalize this to arbitrary 3D rays later. The 2D bounding box is defined by two horizontal and two vertical lines:

$$x = x_0,$$
$$x = x_1,$$
$$y = y_0,$$
$$y = y_1.$$

The points bounded by these lines can be described in interval notation:

$$(x, y) \in [x_0, x_1] \times [y_0, y_1].$$

As shown in Figure 9.5, the intersection test can be phrased in terms of these intervals. First, we compute the ray parameter where the ray hits the line $x = x_{\min}$:

$$t_{x\min} = \frac{x_{\min} - x_e}{x_d}.$$

We then make similar computations for $t_{x\max}$, $t_{y\min}$, and $t_{y\max}$. The ray hits the box if and only if the intervals $[t_{x\min}, t_{x\max}]$ and $[t_{x\min}, t_{x\max}]$ overlap, i.e., their intersection is nonempty. In pseudocode, this algorithm is:

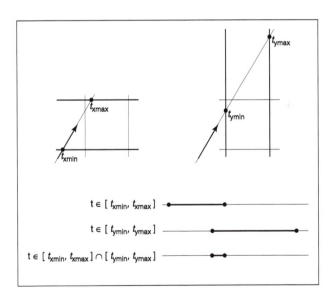

Figure 9.5. The ray will be inside the interval $x \in [x_0, x_1]$ for some interval in its parameter space $t \in [t_{x\min}, t_{x\max}]$. A similar interval exists for the y interval. The ray intersects the box if it is in both the x interval and y interval at the same time, i.e., the intersection of the two one-dimensional intervals is not empty.

$t_{xmin} = (x_0 - x_e)/x_d$
$t_{xmax} = (x_1 - x_e)/x_d$
$t_{ymin} = (y_0 - y_e)/x_d$
$t_{ymax} = (y_1 - y_e)/x_d$
if $(t_{xmin} > t_{ymax})$ *or* $(t_{ymin} > t_{xmax})$ **then**
    return false
else
    return true.

The if statement may seem nonobvious. To see the logic of it, note that there is no overlap if the first interval is either entirely to the right or entirely to the left of the second interval.

The first thing we must address is to account for when x_d or y_d is negative. If x_d is negative, then the ray will hit $x_{\max}$ before it hits $x_{\min}$. Thus, the code for computing t_{xmin} and t_{xmax} would expand to

if $(x_d \geq 0)$ **then**
    $t_{xmin} = (x_0 - x_e)/x_d$
    $t_{xmax} = (x_1 - x_e)/x_d$
else
    $t_{xmin} = (x_1 - x_e)/x_d$
    $t_{xmax} = (x_0 - x_e)/x_d.$

A similar expansion must be made for the y (and z in 3D) cases.

A major concern is that horizontal and vertical rays have a zero value for y_d and x_d, respectively. This will cause divide by zeroes and thus may cause trouble. However, before addressing this directly we should check whether IEEE floating-point computation handles these cases gracefully for us. The rules for divide by zero under IEEE floating point are, for any positive real number a,

$$+a/0 = +\infty$$
$$-a/0 = -\infty.$$

Similarly, for minus zero (allowed by IEEE floating point), we have

$$+a/-0 = -\infty$$
$$-a/+0 = +\infty.$$

Consider the case of a vertical ray where $x_d = 0$ and $y_d > 0$. This gives us

$$t_{\mathrm{xmin}} = \frac{x_0 - x_e}{0}$$
$$t_{\mathrm{xmax}} = \frac{x_1 - x_e}{0}.$$

There are three possibilities of interest:

1. $x_e \leq x_0$ (no hit)

2. $x_0 < x_e < x_1$ (hit)

3. $x_1 \leq x_e$ (no hit).

For the first case, we have

$$t_{\text{xmin}} = \frac{\text{positive number}}{0}$$

$$t_{\text{xmax}} = \frac{\text{positive number}}{0}.$$

This yields the interval $(t_{\text{xmin}}, t_{\text{xmin}}) = (\infty, \infty)$. That interval will not overlap with any interval, so there will be no hit as desired. For the second case, we have

$$t_{\text{xmin}} = \frac{\text{negative number}}{0}$$

$$t_{\text{xmax}} = \frac{\text{positive number}}{0}.$$

This yields the interval $(t_{\text{xmin}}, t_{\text{xmin}}) = (-\infty, \infty)$, which will overlap with all intervals and thus will yield a hit as desired. The third case results in the interval $(-\infty, -\infty)$, which yields no hit as desired. Because these cases work as desired, we need no special checks for them. As is often the case, IEEE floating-point conventions are our ally. However, for $x_d = -0$, things do not work out as desired and we might like to take the other branch in the if. As a way out of this, we note that we can make the if test the value of $1/x_d$ so that the plus and minus zero cases are handled differently. This implies the modification

$a = 1/x_d$
if $(a \geq 0)$ ***then***
    $t_{xmin} = (x_0 - x_e)a$
    $t_{xmax} = (x_1 - x_e)a$
else
    $t_{xmin} = (x_1 - x_e)a$
    $t_{xmax} = (x_0 - x_e)a.$

On some architectures, this will not only solve our -0 problem, but will also improve efficiency because a multiply and two divides is often faster than two divides.

The final optimization for the ray-box test is based on the observation that the value of a and the branch above that is taken is the same for a given ray and every member of the BVH. It is possible to compute these once for a given ray, and this is how we have written our source code.

9.3   C++ CODE

9.3.1   New Ray Class

This ray class precomputes an array of three ints that are determined by the sign of each component of the ray direction. Each element of the *posneg* array is set to zero if the corresponding direction component is postive, or to one if it is negative. These values will be used by the bounding box class in its *rayIntersect* function.

```
// Ray.h

#ifndef _RAY_H_
#define _RAY_H_ 1

#include "Vector3.h"

class Ray
{
public:
    Ray() {}
    Ray(const Vector3& a, const Vector3& b)
    {
        data[0] = a;
        setDirection(b);
    }

    Ray(const Ray& r) {*this = r;}
    Ray& operator=(const Ray& original)
    { setOrigin(original.data[0]); setDirection(original.data[1]); }
    Vector3 origin() const {return data[0];}
    Vector3 direction() const {return data[1];}
    Vector3 invDirection() const {return data[2];}
    void setOrigin(const Vector3& v) {data[0] = v;}
    void setDirection(const Vector3& v)
    {
        data[1] = v;
        data[2] = Vector3(1.0f / v.x(), 1.0f / v.y(), 1.0f / v.z());

        posneg[0] = (data[1].x() > 0 ? 0 : 1);
        posneg[1] = (data[1].y() > 0 ? 0 : 1);
        posneg[2] = (data[1].z() > 0 ? 0 : 1);
    }
```

```
    Vector3 pointAtParameter(float t) const { return data[0] + t*data[1]; }

    Vector3 data[3];
    int posneg[3];
};

#endif // _RAY_H_
```

9.3.2   Axis-Aligned Bounding Box Class

This class uses the ray's *posneg* values to avoid the three checks for positive or
negative directional components.

```
// BBox.h

#ifndef _BBOX_H_
#define _BBOX_H_ 1

#include "Ray.h"

class BBox
{
public:
    BBox() {}
    BBox(const Vector3& a, const Vector3& b) { pp[0] = a; pp[1] = b; }
    Vector3 min() const { return pp[0]; }
    Vector3 max() const { return pp[1]; }
    bool rayIntersect(const Ray& r, float tmin, float tmax) const;

    Vector3 pp[2];
};

inline BBox surround(const BBox& b1, const BBox& b2) {
    return BBox(
 Vector3( b1.min().x() < b2.min().x() ? b1.min().x() : b2.min().x(),
                b1.min().y() < b2.min().y() ? b1.min().y() : b2.min().y(),
                b1.min().z() < b2.min().z() ? b1.min().z() : b2.min().z() ),
         Vector3( b1.max().x() > b2.max().x() ? b1.max().x() : b2.max().x(),
                b1.max().y() > b2.max().y() ? b1.max().y() : b2.max().y(),
                b1.max().z() > b2.max().z() ? b1.max().z() : b2.max().z() ));
}

inline bool BBox::rayIntersect(const Ray& r, float tmin, float tmax) const
{
    float interval_min = tmin;
    float interval_max = tmax;

    int posneg = r.posneg[0];
    float t0 = (pp[posneg].e[0] - r.data[0].e[0]) * r.data[2].e[0];
    float t1 = (pp[1 - posneg].e[0] - r.data[0].e[0]) * r.data[2].e[0];
```

```
    if (t0 > interval_min) interval_min = t0;
    if (t1 < interval_max) interval_max = t1;
    if (interval_min > interval_max) return false;

    posneg = r.posneg[1];
    t0 = (pp[posneg].e[1] - r.data[0].e[1]) * r.data[2].e[1];
    t1 = (pp[1 - posneg].e[1] - r.data[0].e[1]) * r.data[2].e[1];
    if (t0 > interval_min) interval_min = t0;
    if (t1 < interval_max) interval_max = t1;
    if (interval_min > interval_max) return false;

    posneg = r.posneg[2];
    t0 = (pp[posneg].e[2] - r.data[0].e[2]) * r.data[2].e[2];
    t1 = (pp[1 - posneg].e[2] - r.data[0].e[2]) * r.data[2].e[2];
    if (t0 > interval_min) interval_min = t0;
    if (t1 < interval_max) interval_max = t1;
    return (interval_min <= interval_max);
}

#endif // _BBOX_H_
```

9.3.3   Partitioning Routine

```
// qsplit.h

#ifndef _QSPLIT_H_
#define _QSPLIT_H_ 1

#include "Shape.h"
#include "BBox.h"

int qsplit(Shape** list, int size, float pivot_val, int axis)
{
    BBox bbox;
    double centroid;
    int ret_val = 0;

    for (int i = 0; i < size; i++)
    {
        bbox = list[i]->boundingBox(0.0f, 0.0f);
        centroid = ((bbox.min())[axis] + (bbox.max())[axis]) / 2.0f;
        if (centroid < pivot_val)
        {
            Shape* temp = list[i];
            list[i]      = list[ret_val];
            list[ret_val] = temp;
            ret_val++;
        }
    }
    if (ret_val == 0 || ret_val == size) ret_val = size/2;

    return ret_val;
```

```
}

#endif // _QSPLIT_H_
```

9.3.4 Bounding Volume Hierarchy

This is a simple implementation of a BVH class. Additional optimizations can be attempted, but we have found that this simple algorithm is difficult to improve upon. One promising effort is to store the splitting plane position along with each interior node and use this to determine which side of the splitting plane the ray is on. We can then test the nearest child first, hoping for early termination in the far child.

```
#ifndef _BVH_H_
#define _BVH_H_

#include "Shape.h"
#include "BBox.h"

class BVH : public Shape
{
public:
    BVH();
    BVH(Shape** surfaces, int num_surfaces);
    BVH(Shape* prim1, Shape* prim2);
    BVH(Shape* prim1, Shape* prim2, const BBox& _bbox);
    bool hit(const Ray& r, float tmin, float tmax, float time,
    HitRecord& rec)const;
    bool shadowHit(const Ray& r, float tmin, float tmax, float time) const;
    BBox boundingBox( float time0, float time1 )const;
    Shape* buildBranch (Shape** surfaces, int num_surfaces, int axis = 0);

    BBox bbox;
    Shape* left;
    Shape* right;
};

inline BVH::BVH(Shape* prim1, Shape* prim2, const BBox& _bbox) {
    bbox = _bbox;
    left  = prim1;
    right = prim2;
}
inline BVH::BVH(Shape* prim1, Shape* prim2) {
    left  = prim1;
    right = prim2;
    bbox = surround(prim1->boundingBox(0.0f, 0.0f),
                    prim2->boundingBox(0.0f, 0.0f));
}

#endif // _BVH_H_
```

```
// BVH.cc

#include "BVH.h"
#include "qsplit.h"

BVH::BVH() {}

BVH::BVH(Shape** shapes, int num_shapes)
{
    if (num_shapes == 1) *this = BVH(shapes[0], shapes[0]);
    if (num_shapes == 2) *this = BVH(shapes[0], shapes[1]);

    // find the midpoint of the bounding box to use as a qsplit pivot
    bbox = shapes[0]->boundingBox(0.0f, 0.0f);
    for (int i = 1; i < num_shapes; i++)
        bbox = surround(bbox, shapes[i]->boundingBox(0.0f, 0.0f));
    Vector3 pivot = (bbox.max() + bbox.min()) / 2.0f;

    int mid_point = qsplit(shapes, num_shapes, pivot.x(), 0);

    // create a new boundingVolume
    left  = buildBranch(shapes, mid_point, 1);
    right = buildBranch(&shapes[mid_point], num_shapes - mid_point, 1);
}

BBox BVH::boundingBox( float time0, float time1 )const
{ return bbox; }

bool BVH::hit(const Ray& r, float tmin, float tmax, float time,
        HitRecord& rec)const
{
    if (!(bbox.rayIntersect(r, tmin, tmax))) return false;

    // else call hit on both branches
    bool isahit1 = false;
    bool isahit2 = false;
    rec.t = tmax;

    isahit1 = right->hit(r, tmin, tmax, time, rec);
    isahit2 = left->hit(r, tmin, rec.t, time, rec);

    return (isahit1 || isahit2);
}

bool BVH::shadowHit(const Ray& r, float tmin, float tmax, float time) const
{
    if (!(bbox.rayIntersect(r, tmin, tmax))) return false;

    if (right->shadowHit(r, tmin, tmax, time)) return true;
    return  left->shadowHit(r, tmin, tmax, time);
}

Shape* BVH::buildBranch (Shape** shapes, int shape_size, int axis)
```

```
{
    if (shape_size == 1) return shapes[0];
    if (shape_size == 2) return new BVH(shapes[0], shapes[1]);

    // find the midpoint of the bounding box to use as a qsplit pivot
    BBox box = shapes[0]->boundingBox(0.0f, 0.0f);
    for (int i = 1; i < shape_size; i++)
        box = surround(box, shapes[i]->boundingBox(0.0f, 0.0f));

    Vector3 pivot = (box.max() + box.min()) / 2.0f;

    // now split according to correct axis
    int mid_point = qsplit(shapes, shape_size, pivot[axis], axis);

    // create a new boundingVolume
    Shape* left  = buildBranch(shapes, mid_point, (axis + 1) % 3);
    Shape* right = buildBranch(&shapes[mid_point], shape_size-mid_point,
    (axis+1)%3);
    return new BVH(left, right, box);
}
```

9.4 NOTES

Various efficiency structures are surveyed in *An Introduction to Raytracing* (edited by Glassner, Academic Press, 1989). Efficency startegies and tradeoffs are discussed in "Efficiency Issues for Ray Tracing" (Smits, *Journal of Graphics Tools*, 1998). The bounding-box intersection routine presented in this chapter is from "An Efficient and Robust Ray-Box Intersection Algorithm" (Williams et al., *Journal of Graphics Tools*, to appear). The *qsplit* routine presented in this chapter is based on code by Brandon Mansfield.

10 | Monte Carlo Integration

The previous chapters covered the geometric aspects of a ray tracing program. What is left is *lighting*, so that our images can start looking rich from shading effects. To implement this we need to use *Monte Carlo integration*. This requires covering some hairy-looking math, but the resulting program will be quite clean.

10.1 INTEGRALS

Although the word "integral" often seems to intimidate students, it is one of the most intuitive concepts found in mathematics, and it should not be feared. For our very nonrigorous purposes, an integral is just a function that maps subsets to $\mathbb{R}^+$ (the nonnegative real numbers) in a manner consistent with our intuitive notions of length, area, and volume. For example, on the 2D real plane $\mathbb{R}^2$, an integral of a region is just the area of that region. The worst thing about integration is that it has somewhat ugly notation. For example, the area of a set S is:

$$A(S) \equiv \int_{x \in S} dA(\mathbf{x}).$$

You can informally read the right-hand side as "take all points $\mathbf{x}$ in the region S, and sum their associated differential areas." The integral is often written other ways, including:

$$\int_S dA,$$

$$\int_{\mathbf{x} \in S} d\mathbf{x},$$

$$\int_{\mathbf{x} \in S} dA_{\mathbf{x}},$$

$$\int_{\mathbf{x}} d\mathbf{x}.$$

All of the above formulas can be read at a high level as "the area of region S." We will stick with the first "reading" we used because it is so verbose it avoids ambiguity. To evaluate such integrals analytically, we usually need to lay down some coordinate system and use our bag of calculus tricks to solve the equations. But have no fear if those skills have faded as we usually have to numerically approximate integrals using Monte Carlo integration.

10.2   CONTINUOUS PROBABILITY

Before we approximate integrals, we will need some tools to construct and characterize random samples. This is the domain of applied continuous probability.

10.2.1   One-Dimensional Continuous Probability Density Functions

Loosely speaking, a *continuous random variable* x is a scalar or vector quantity that "randomly" takes on a value on the real line $\mathbb{R} = (-\infty, +\infty)$. The behavior of x is entirely described by the distribution of values it takes. This distribution of values can be quantitatively described by the *probability density function*, p, associated with x (the relationship is denoted $x \sim p$). The probability that x will take on a value in some interval $[a, b]$ is given by the integral:

$$\text{Probability}(x \in [a, b]) = \int_a^b p(x)dx. \tag{10.1}$$

Loosely speaking, the probability density function p describes the relative likelihood of a random variable taking a certain value; if $p(x_1) = 6.0$ and $p(x_2) = 3.0$, then a random variable with density p is twice as likely to have a value "near" x_1 than it is to have a value near x_2. The density p has two characteristics:

$$p(x) \geq 0 \quad \text{(Probability is nonnegative)}, \tag{10.2}$$

$$\int_{-\infty}^{+\infty} p(x)dx = 1 \quad (\text{Probability}(x \in \mathbb{R}) = 1). \tag{10.3}$$

As an example, the *canonical* random variable ξ takes on values between zero (inclusive) and one (noninclusive) with uniform probability (here *uniform* simply means each value for ξ is equally likely). This implies that the probability density function q for ξ is:

$$q(\xi) = \begin{cases} 1 & \text{if } 0 \leq \xi < 1 \\ 0 & \text{otherwise.} \end{cases}$$

The space over which ξ is defined is simply the interval $[0, 1)$. The probability that ξ takes on a value in a certain interval $[a, b] \in [0, 1)$ is:

$$\text{Probability}(a \leq \xi \leq b) = \int_a^b 1 \, dx = b - a.$$

10.2.2 One-Dimensional Expected Value

The average value that a real function f of a one-dimensional random variable with underlying pdf (probability distribution function) p will take on is called its *expected value*, $E(f(x))$ (sometimes written $Ef(x)$):

$$E(f(x)) = \int f(x)p(x)dx.$$

The expected value of a one-dimensional random variable can be calculated by letting $f(x) = x$. The expected value has a surprising and useful property: the expected value of the sum of two random variables is the sum of the expected values of those variables:

$$E(x + y) = E(x) + E(y),$$

for random variables x and y. Because functions of random variables are themselves random variables, this linearity of expectation applies to them as well:

$$E(f(x) + g(y)) = E(f(x)) + E(g(y)).$$

An obvious question is whether this property holds if the random variables being summed are correlated (variables that are not correlated are called *independent*). This linearity property in fact does hold *whether or not* the variables are independent! This summation property is vital for most Monte Carlo applications.

10.2.3 Multi-Dimensional Random Variables

The discussion of random variables and their expected values extends naturally to multidimensional spaces. Most graphics problems will be in such higher-dimensional spaces. For example, many lighting problems are phrased on the surface of the hemisphere. Fortunately, if we define a measure μ on the space the random variables occupy, everything is very similar to the one-dimensional case. Suppose the space S has associated measure μ; for example, S is the surface of a sphere and μ measures area. We can define a pdf $p : S \mapsto \mathbb{R}$, and if x is a random variable with $x \sim p$, then the probability that x will take on a value in some region $S_i \subset S$ is given by the integral:

$$\text{Probability}(x \in S_i) = \int_{S_i} p(x)d\mu.$$

Here *Probability(event)* is the probability that the *event* is true, so the integral is the probability that x takes on a value in the region S_i.

In graphics, S is often an area ($d\mu = dA = dxdy$), or a set of directions (points on a unit sphere: $d\mu = d\omega = \sin\theta\, d\theta\, d\phi$). As an example, a two-dimensional random variable α is a uniformly distributed random variable on a disk of radius R. Here *uniformly* means uniform with respect to area, e.g., the way a bad dart player's hits would be distributed on a dart board. Since it is uniform, we know that $p(\alpha)$ is some constant. From the fact that the area of the disk is πr^2 and that the total probability is one, we can deduce that:

$$p(\alpha) = \frac{1}{\pi R^2}.$$

This means that the probability that α is in a certain subset S_1 of the disk is just:

$$\text{Probability}(\alpha \in S_1) = \int_{S_1} \frac{1}{\pi R^2} dA.$$

This is all very abstract. To actually use this information, we need the integral in a form we can evaluate. Suppose S_i is the portion of the disk closer to the center than the perimeter. If we convert to polar coordinates, then α is represented as a (r, ϕ) pair, and S_1 is where $r < R/2$. Note that just because α is uniform does not imply that θ or r are necessarily uniform (in fact, θ is, and r is not). The differential area dA becomes $r\, dr\, d\phi$. This leads to:

$$\text{Probability}\left(r < \frac{R}{2}\right) = \int_0^{2\pi} \int_0^{\frac{R}{2}} \frac{1}{\pi R^2} r\, dr\, d\phi = 0.25.$$

The formula for expected value of a real function applies to the multidimensional case:

$$E(f(x)) = \int_S f(x)p(x)d\mu,$$

where $x \in S$ and $f : S \mapsto \mathbb{R}$, and $p : S \mapsto \mathbb{R}$. For example, on the unit square $S = [0,1] \times [0,1]$ and $p(x,y) = 4xy$, the expected value of the x coordinate for

$(x, y) \sim p$ is:

$$E(x) = \int_S f(x, y)p(x, y)dA$$

$$= \int_0^1 \int_0^1 4x^2y \; dx \; dy$$

$$= \frac{2}{3}.$$

Note that here, $f(x, y) = x$.

10.2.4   Estimated Means

Many problems involve sums of independent random variables x_i, where the variables share a common density p. Such variables are said to be *independent identically distributed* (iid) random variables. When the sum is divided by the number of variables, we get an estimate of $E(x)$:

$$E(x) \approx \frac{1}{N} \sum_{i=1}^{N} x_i.$$

As N increases, the expected error of this estimate decreases. We want N to be large enough that we have confidence that the estimate is "close enough." However, there are no sure things in Monte Carlo; we just gain statistical confidence that our estimate is good. To be sure, we would have to have $n = \infty$. This confidence is expressed by *Law of Large Numbers*:

$$\text{Probability} \left[E(x) = \lim_{N \to \infty} \frac{1}{N} \sum_{i=1}^{N} x_i \right] = 1.$$

10.3   MONTE CARLO INTEGRATION

In this section, the basic Monte Carlo solution methods for definite integrals are outlined. These techniques are then straightforwardly applied to certain integral problems. All of the basic material of this section is also covered in several of the classic Monte Carlo texts.

As discussed earlier, given a function $f : S \mapsto \mathbb{R}$ and a random variable $x \sim p$, we can approximate the expected value of $f(x)$ by a sum:

$$E(f(x)) = \int_{x \in S} f(x)p(x)d\mu \approx \frac{1}{N} \sum_{i=1}^{N} f(x_i). \tag{10.4}$$

Because the expected value can be expressed as an integral, the integral is also approximated by the sum. The form of Equation 10.4 is a bit awkward; we would usually like to approximate an integral of a single function g rather than a product fp. We can get around this by substituting $g = fp$ as the integrand:

$$\int_{x \in S} g(x)d\mu \approx \frac{1}{N} \sum_{i=1}^{N} \frac{g(x_i)}{p(x_i)}. \tag{10.5}$$

For this formula to be valid, p must be positive where g is nonzero.

So to get a good estimate, we want as many samples as possible, and we want the g/p to have a low variance (g and p should have a similar shape). Choosing p intelligently is called *importance sampling*, because if p is large where g is large, there will be more samples in important regions. Equation 10.4 also shows the fundamental problem with Monte Carlo integration: *diminishing return*. Because the variance of the estimate is proportional to $1/N$, the standard deviation is proportional to $1/\sqrt{N}$. Since the error in the estimate behaves similarly to the standard deviation, we will need to quadruple N to halve the error.

Another way to reduce variance is to partition S, the domain of the integral, into several smaller domains S_i, and evaluate the integral as a sum of integrals over the S_i. This is called *stratified sampling*, the technique that jittering employs in pixel sampling (see Chapter 3). Normally only one sample is taken in each S_i (with density p_i), and in this case, the expected error of the estimate is:

$$var \left(\sum_{i=1}^{N} \frac{g(x_i)}{p_i(x_i)} \right) = \sum_{i=1}^{N} var \left(\frac{g(x_i)}{p_i(x_i)} \right). \tag{10.6}$$

It can be shown that the expected error of stratified sampling is never higher than unstratified if all strata have equal measure:

$$\int_{S_i} p(x)d\mu = \frac{1}{N} \int_{S} p(x)d\mu.$$

The most common example of stratified sampling in graphics is jittering for pixel sampling as discussed in Chapter 3.

As an example of the Monte Carlo solution of an integral I, set $g(x)$ to be x over the interval $(0, 4)$:

$$I = \int_{0}^{4} x\,dx = 8. \tag{10.7}$$

Note that the expected error is lessened when the shape of p is similar to the shape of g. The expected error drops to zero if $p = g/I$, but I is not usually known or we would not have to resort to Monte Carlo. One important principle is that stratified sampling is often *far* superior to importance sampling. However, using both in conjunction is best.

10.4 CHOOSING RANDOM POINTS

We often want to generate sets of random or pseudorandom points on the unit square for tasks such as sampling pixels. There are several methods for doing this such as jittering (see Chapter 3). hese methods give us a set of N reasonably equidistributed points on the unit square $[0, 1]^2 : (u_1, v_1)$ through (u_N, v_N).

Sometimes, our sampling space may not be square (e.g., a circular lens), or may not be uniform (e.g, the filter function centered on a pixel we saw in Chapter 3). It would be nice if we could write a mathematical transformation that would take our equidistributed points (u_i, v_i) as input, and output a set of points in our desired sampling space with our desired density (we did this for cubic filters in Chapter 3, but we didn't justify our mapping). For example, to sample a camera lens, the transformation would take (u_i, v_i) and output (r_i, ϕ_i) such that the new points were approximately equidistributed on the disk of the lens. While we might be tempted to use the transform:

$$\phi_i = 2\pi u_i,$$
$$r_i = v_i R,$$

it has a serious problem. While the points do cover the lens, they do so nonuniformly (Figure 10.1, left). What we need in this case is a transformation that takes equal-area regions to equal-area regions. That will take uniform sampling distributions on the square to uniform distributions on the new domain.

10.4.1 Function Inversion

If the density is a one-dimensional $f(x)$ defined over the interval $x \in [x_{min}, x_{max}]$, then we can generate random numbers α_i that have density f from a set of uniform random numbers ξ_i, where $\xi_i \in [0, 1]$. To do this we need the cumulative probability distribution function $P(x)$:

$$\text{Probability}(\alpha < x) = P(x) = \int_{x_{min}}^{x} f(x')d\mu.$$

To get α_i. we simply transform ξ_i:

$$\alpha_i = P^{-1}(\xi_i)$$

where P^{-1} is the inverse of P. If P is not analytically invertible, then numerical methods will suffice because an inverse exists for all valid probability distribution functions.

Note that analytically inverting a function is more confusing than it should be, due to notation. For example, if we have the function

$$y = x^2,$$

for $x > 0$, then the inverse function is just in terms of y as a function of x:

$$x = \sqrt{y}.$$

When the function is analytically invertible, it is almost always that simple. However, things are a little more opaque with the standard notation:

$$f(x) = x^2,$$
$$f^{-1}(x) = \sqrt{x}.$$

Here x is just a dummy variable. You may find it easier to use the less standard notation:

$$y = x^2,$$
$$x = \sqrt{y},$$

while keeping in mind these are inverse functions of each other.

For example, to choose random points x_i that have the density

$$p(x) = \frac{3x^2}{2}$$

on $[-1, 1]$, we see that

$$P(x) = \frac{x^3 + 1}{2},$$

and

$$P^{-1}(x) = \sqrt[3]{2x - 1},$$

so we can "warp" a set of canonical random numbers $(\xi_1, \cdots, \xi_N)$ to the properly distributed numbers

$$(x_1, \cdots, x_N) = (\sqrt[3]{2\xi_1 - 1}, \cdots, \sqrt[3]{2\xi_N - 1}).$$

Of course, this same warping function can be used to transform "uniform" jittered samples into nicely distributed samples with the desired density.

If we have a random variable $\alpha = (\alpha_x, \alpha_y)$ with two-dimensional density (x, y) defined on $[x_{min}, x_{max}] \times [y_{min}, y_{max}]$ then we need the two-dimensional distribution function:

$$\text{Probability}(\alpha_x < x \text{ and } \alpha_y < y) = F(x, y) = \int_{y_{min}}^{y} \int_{x_{min}}^{x} f(x', y') d\mu(x', y').$$

We first choose an x_i using the marginal distribution $F(x, y_{max})$, and then choose y_i according to $F(x_i, y)/F(x_i, y_{max})$. If $f(x, y)$ is separable (expressible as $g(x)h(y)$), then the one-dimensional techniques can be used on each dimension.

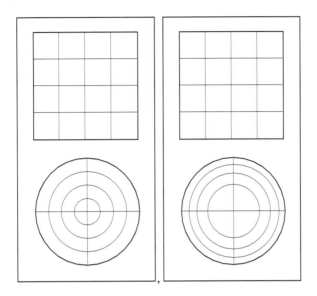

Figure 10.1. Left: The transform that takes the horizontal and vertical dimensions uniformly to (r, ϕ) does not preserve relative area; not all of the resulting areas are the same. Right: An area-preserving map.

Returning to our earlier example, suppose we are sampling uniformly from the disk of radius R, so $p(r, \phi) = 1/(\pi R^2)$. The two-dimensional distribution function is:

$$\text{Probability}(r < r_0 \text{ and } \phi < \phi_0) = F(r_0, \phi_0) = \int_0^{\phi_0} \int_0^{r_0} \frac{r\, dr\, d\phi}{\pi R^2} = \frac{\phi r^2}{2\pi R^2}.$$

This means that a canonical pair (ξ_1, ξ_2) can be transformed to a uniform random point on the disk:

$$\phi = 2\pi \xi_1,$$
$$r = R\sqrt{\xi_2}.$$

This mapping is shown in Figure 10.1.

To choose reflected ray directions for some realistic rendering applications, we choose points on the unit hemisphere according to the density:

$$p(\theta, \phi) = \frac{n+1}{2\pi} \cos^n \theta, \tag{10.8}$$

where n is a Phong-like exponent, θ is the angle from the surface normal and $\theta \in [0, \pi/2]$ (on the upper hemisphere), and ϕ is the azimuthal angle ($\phi \in [0, 2\pi]$).

The cumulative distribution function is:

$$P(\theta, \phi) = \int_0^\phi \int_0^\theta p(\theta', \phi') \sin \theta' d\theta' d\phi'. \tag{10.9}$$

The $\cos \theta'$ term arises because on the sphere, $d\omega = \cos \theta d\theta d\phi$. When the marginal densities are found, p (as expected) is separable and we find that a (ξ_1, ξ_2) pair of canonical random numbers can be transformed to a direction by:

$$\theta = \arccos \left((1 - r_1)^{\frac{1}{n+1}} \right)$$

$$\phi = 2\pi r_2$$

.

Again, a nice thing about this is that a set of jittered points on the unit square can be easily transformed to a set of jittered points on the hemisphere with the desired distribution. Note that if n is set to 1, then we have a diffuse distribution as is often needed.

Often we must map the point on the sphere into an appropriate direction with respect to a uvw basis. To do this, we can first convert the angles to a unit vector a:

$$\mathbf{a} = (\cos \phi \sin \theta, \; \sin \phi \sin \theta, \; \cos \theta).$$

As an efficiency improvement, you can avoid taking trigonometric functions of inverse trigonometric functions (e.g. $\cos \arccos \theta$). For example, when $n = 1$ (a diffuse distribution), the vector $\vec{a}$ simplifies to

$$\mathbf{a} = \left(\cos \left(2\pi\xi_1 \right) \sqrt{\xi_2}, \sin \left(2\pi\xi_1 \right) \sqrt{\xi_2}, \sqrt{1 - \xi_2} \right).$$

10.5 NOTES

Monte Carlo methods for graphics are discussed in "Monte Carlo Rendering" (Jensen, in SIGGRAPH Course Notes, 2003). Some convergence properties of stratified sampling in graphics is given in "Consequences of Stratified Sampling in Graphics" (Mitchell, in *Computer Graphics (Proc. SIGGRAPH '96)*, 1996).

11 | Radiometry

Before we add lighting to our ray tracer, we need to precisely say what "how much" means when we are discussing light. In this chapter we discuss the practical issues of measuring light, an endeavor usually called *radiometry*. The terms that arise in radiometry may at first seem strange, and its terminology and notation may be hard to keep straight. However, because radiometry is so fundamental to computer graphics, it is worth studying radiometry until it sinks in.

Although we can define radiometric units in many systems, we use the *SI* units. Familiar *SI* units include the familiar metric units of meter (m) and gram (g). Light is fundamentally a propagating form of energy, so it is useful to define the *SI* unit of energy which is the Joule (J). We discuss how quantities vary with the wavelength of light. However, in our implementation, we use RGB color. You can think of RGB as three different wavelengths for the purposes of intuition.

11.1 PHOTONS

To aid intuition, we will describe radiometry in terms of collections of large numbers of *photons*, and this section establishes what is meant by a photon in this context. For the purposes of this chapter, a photon is a quantum of light that has a position, direction of propagation, and a wavelength λ. Somewhat strangely, the *SI* unit used for wavelength is *nanometer* (nm). This is mainly for historical reasons, and $1nm = 10^{-9}m$. Another unit, the *angstrom,* is sometimes used; one nanometer is ten angstroms. A photon also has a speed c that depends only on the refractive index n of the medium through which it propagates. Sometimes the frequency $f = c/\lambda$ is also used for light. This is convenient because unlike λ and c, f does not change when the photon refracts into a medium with a new refractive index. Another invariant is the amount of energy q carried by a photon, which is given by the following relationship:

$$q = hf = \frac{hc}{\lambda},$$
(11.1)

where $h = 6.63 \times 10^{-34} Js$ is Planck's constant. Although these quantities can be measured using many unit systems, we use *SI* units whenever possible.

11.2 SPECTRAL ENERGY

If we have a large collection of photons, their total energy Q can be computed by summing the energy q_i of each photon. A reasonable question to ask is, "how is the energy distributed across wavelengths?" An easy way to answer this is to partition the photons into bins, essentially histogramming them. You would then have an energy associated with an interval. For example, you might count all the energy between $\lambda = 500nm$ and $\lambda = 600nm$, and have it turn out to be $10.2J$. This might be denoted $q[500, 600] = 10.2$. If we divided the wavelength interval into two $50nm$ intervals, we might find that $q[500, 550] = 5.2$ and $q[550, 600] = 5.0$. This tells us there was a little more energy in the short wavelength half of the interval $[500, 600]$. If we divide into $25nm$ bins, we might find $q[500, 525] = 2.5$ and so on. The nice thing about the system is that it is straightforward. The bad thing about it is that the choice of the interval size determines the number.

A more commonly used system is to divide the energy by the size of the interval. So instead of $q[500, 600] = 10.2$, we would have:

$$Q_\lambda[500, 600] = \frac{10.2}{100} = 0.12 J(nm)^{-1}.$$

This is nice because the size of the interval has much less impact on the overall size of the numbers. An immediate idea would be to drive the interval size $\Delta\lambda$ to zero. This would be awkward because for a sufficiently small $\Delta\lambda$, Q_λ will either be zero or huge depending on whether there is a single photon or no photon in the interval. There are two schools of thought to solve that dilemma. The first is to assume that $\Delta\lambda$ is small, but not so small that the quantum nature of light comes into play. The second is to assume that the light is a continuum rather than individual photons, so a true derivative $dQ/d\lambda$ is appropriate. Both ways of thinking about it are appropriate and lead to the same computational machinery. In practice, it seems that most people who measure light prefer small but finite intervals because that is what they can measure in the lab. Most people that do theory or computation prefer infinitesimal intervals because that makes the machinery of calculus available.

The quantity Q_λ is called *spectral energy* and is an *intensive* quantity. This is opposed to an *extensive* quantity such as energy, length, or mass. Intensive quantities can be thought of as density functions that tell you the density of an extensive quantity at an infinitesimal point. For example, the energy Q at a specific wavelength is probably zero, but the spectral energy (energy density) Q_λ is a meaningful quantity. A probably more familiar example is that the population of a country may be 25 million, but the population at a point in that country is meaningless. However, the population *density* measured in people per square meter is meaningful provided it is measured over large enough areas. Much like with photons, population density works best if we pretend that we can view population as a continuum where population density never becomes granular, even when the area is small.

We will follow the convention of graphics where spectral energy is almost always used, and energy is rarely used. This results in a proliferation of λ subscripts if "proper" notation is used. Instead, we will drop the subscript and use Q to denote spectral energy. This can result in some confusion when people outside of graphics read graphics papers, so be aware of this standards issue. Your intuition about spectral power might be aided by imagining a measurement device with an energy sensor that measures light energy q. If you place a colored filter in front of the sensor that allows only light in the interval $[\lambda - \Delta\lambda/2, \lambda + \Delta\lambda/2]$, then the spectral power at λ would be $Q = \Delta q/\Delta\lambda$.

11.3 POWER

It is useful to estimate a rate of energy production for light sources. This rate is called *power* and is measured in *Watts* W, which is another name for *Joules per second*. This is easiest to understand in a *steady state*, but because power is an intensive quantity (a density over time): it is well defined even when energy production is varying over time. The units of power may be more familiar because of lights, e.g., a 100 watt light bulb. Such bulbs draw approximately $100J$ of energy each second. The power of the light produced will be lower than $100W$ because of heat loss, etc., but that can still be used to help intuition. For example, we can get a feel for how many photons are produced in second by a $100W$ light. Suppose the average photon produced has the energy of a $\lambda = 500nm$ photon. The frequency of such a photon is:

$$f = \frac{c}{\lambda} = \frac{3 \times 10^8 ms^{-1}}{500 \times 10^{-9} m} = 6 \times 10^{14} s^{-1}.$$

The energy of that photon is $hf \approx 4 \times 10^{-19} J$. That means a staggering 10^{20} photons are produced each second even if the bulb is not very efficient. This explains why simulating a camera with a fast shutter speed and directly simulated photons is an inefficient choice for producing images.

As with energy, we are really interested in *spectral power* measured in $W(nm)^{-1}$. Again, although the formal standard symbol for spectral power is Φ_λ, we will use Φ with no subscript for convenience and consistency with most of the graphics literature. One thing to note is that the spectral power for a light source is usually a smaller number than the power. For example, if a light emits a power of $100W$ evenly distributed over wavelengths $400nm$ to $800nm$, then the spectral power will be $100W/400nm = .25W\,(nm)^{-1}$. This is something to keep in mind if you set the spectral power of light sources by hand for debugging purposes.

The measurement device for spectral energy in the last section could be modified by taking a reading with a shutter that is open for a time interval Δt centered at time t. The spectral power would then be $\Delta Q/(\Delta t\Delta\lambda)$.

11.4 IRRADIANCE

The quantity *irradiance* arises naturally if you ask the question, "How much light hits this point?" Of course the answer is "none" and again we must use a density function. If the point is on a surface, it is natural to use area to define our density function. We modify the device from the last section to have a finite ΔA area sensor that is smaller than the light field being measured. The spectral irradiance H would just be the power per unit area $\Delta\Phi/\Delta A$. Fully expanded, this is:

$$\Phi = \frac{\Delta q}{\Delta A\,\Delta t\Delta\lambda}. \tag{11.2}$$

Thus the full units of irradiance are $Jm^{-2}s^{-1}(nm)^{-1}$. Note that it is *not* $Jm^{-3}s$. This is a perversity introduced by using square meters for area and nanometers for wavelength, but it is standard radiometry.

When the light is leaving a surface, e.g., when it is reflected, the same quantity as irradiance is called *radiant exitance E*. It is useful to have different words for incident and exitant light because the same point has potentially different irradiance and radiant exitance.

11.5 RADIANCE

Although radiant exitance tells us how much light is arriving at a point, it tells us little about the direction that light comes from. To measure something analogous to what we see with our eyes, we need to be able to associate "how much light" with a specific direction. Before we do this, we need to associate a "size" with a direction. This is *solid angle* as illustrated in Figure 11.1. The solid angle is similar in spirit to an angle, but rather than the length of an arc on the unit circle it is the area of a region on the unit sphere. This measure is in *steradians*, which can be anywhere from zero to 4π (the area of the unit sphere) for various solid angles. One way to visualize solid angles is to think of how big something looks in your visual field as opposed to its actual area without the projection.

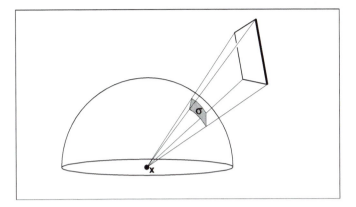

Figure 11.1. The solid angle subtended by a surface is its projected area σ on the unit sphere centered at the viewpoint.

We can imagine a simple device to measure such a quantity (Figure 11.2). We use a small irradiance meter and add on conical "baffler" which limits light hitting the counter to a range of angles with solid angle $\Delta\sigma$. The response of the detector is thus:

$$\text{response} = \frac{\Delta H}{\Delta\sigma}$$
$$= \frac{\Delta q}{\Delta A\,\Delta\sigma\,\Delta t\,\Delta\lambda}.$$

This is the spectral *radiance* of light traveling in space. Again, we will drop the "spectral" in our discussion and assume that it is implicit.

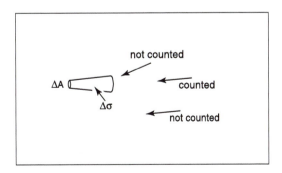

Figure 11.2. By adding a blinder that shows only a small solid angle $\Delta\sigma$ to the irradiance detector, we measure radiance.

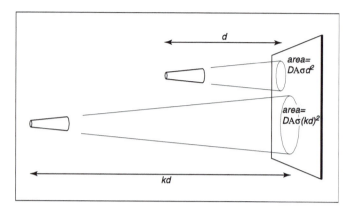

Figure 11.3. The signal a radiance detector receives does not depend on distance to the surface being measured. This figure assumes the detectors are pointing at areas on the surface that are emitting light in the same way.

Radiance is what we are usually computing in graphics programs. A wonderful property of radiance is that it does not vary along a line in space. To see why this is true, examine the two radiances both looking at a surface as shown in Figure 11.3. Assume the lines the detectors are looking along are close enough together that the surface is emitting/reflecting light "the same" in both of the areas being measured. Because the area of the surface being sampled is proportional to squared distance, and because the light reaching the detector is *inversely* proportional to squared distance, the two detectors should have the same reading.

It is useful to measure the radiance hitting a surface. We can think of placing the cone baffler from the radiance detector at a point on the surface and measuring the irradiance H on the surface originating from directions in the cone (Figure 11.4). Note that the surface "detector" is not aligned with the cone. For this reason, we need to add a cosine correction term to our definition of radiance:

$$\text{response} = \frac{\Delta H}{\Delta \sigma \cos \theta}$$

$$= \frac{\Delta q}{\Delta A \cos \theta \, \Delta \sigma \, \Delta t \, \Delta \lambda}.$$

As with irradiance and radiant exitance, it is useful to distinguish between radiance incident at a point on a surface and exitant from that point. Terms for these concepts sometimes used in the graphics literature are *surface radiance* L_s for the radiance of (leaving) a surface, and *field radiance* for the radiance incident at a surface. Both have the cosine term because they both correspond to the

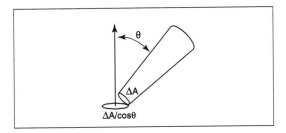

Figure 11.4. The irradiance at the surface as masked by the cone is smaller than that measured at the detector by a cosine factor.

configuration in Figure 11.4:

$$L_s = \frac{\Delta E}{\Delta\sigma \cos\theta}$$
$$L_f = \frac{\Delta H}{\Delta\sigma \cos\theta}.$$

11.5.1 Deriving Other Radiometric Quantities from Radiance

If we have a surface whose field radiance is L_f, then we can derive all of the other radiometric quantities from it. This is one reason radiance is considered the "fundamental" radiometric quantity. For example, the irradiance is:

$$H = \int_{\text{all } \mathbf{k}} L_f(\mathbf{k}) \, \cos\theta \, d\sigma.$$

This formula has several notational conventions that are common in graphics that make such formulae opaque to readers not familiar with them (Figure 11.5). First, $\mathbf{k}$ is an incident direction, and can be thought of as a unit vector, a direction, or a (θ, ϕ) pair in spherical coordinates with respect to the surface normal. The direction has a differential solid angle $d\sigma$ associated with it. The field radiance is potentially different for every direction, so we write it as a function $L(\mathbf{k})$.

As an example, we can compute the irradiance H at a surface that has constant field radiance L_f in all directions. To integrate, we use a classic spherical coordinate system, and recall that the differential solid angle is

$$d\sigma \equiv \sin\theta \, d\theta \, d\phi$$

so the irradiance is:

$$H = \int_{\phi=0}^{2\pi} \int_{\theta=0}^{\frac{\pi}{2}} L_f \, \cos\theta \, \sin\theta \, d\theta \, d\phi$$
$$= \pi L_f.$$

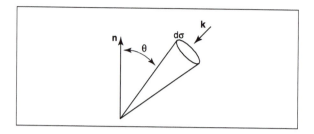

Figure 11.5. The direction **k** has a differential solid angle $d\sigma$ associated with it.

This relation shows us our first occurrence of a potentially surprising constant π. These factors of π occur frequently in radiometry and are an artifact of how we chose to measure solid angles, i.e., the area of a unit sphere is a multiple of π rather than a multiple of one.

Similarly, we can find the power hitting a surface by integrating the irradiance across the surface area:

$$\Phi = \int_{\text{all } \mathbf{x}} H(\mathbf{x}) dA,$$

where $\mathbf{x}$ is a point on the surface, and dA is the differential area associated with that point. Note that we don't have special terms of symbols for incoming versus outgoing power. That distinction does not seem to come up enough to have encouraged the distinction.

11.6 BRDF

Because we are interested in surface appearance, we would like to characterize how a surface reflects light. At an intuitive level, for any incident light coming from direction $\mathbf{k}_i$, there is some fraction scattered in a small solid angle near outgoing direction $\mathbf{k}_o$. There are many ways we could formalize such a concept, and not surprisingly, the standard way to do so is inspired by building a simple measurement device. Such a device is shown in Figure 11.6, where a small light source is positioned in direction $\mathbf{k}_i$ as seen from a point on a surface, and a detector is placed in direction $\mathbf{k}_o$. For every directional pair $(\mathbf{k}_i, \mathbf{k}_o)$, we take a reading with the detector.

Now we just have to decide how to measure the strength of the light source and make our reflection function independent of this strength. For example, if we replaced the light with a brighter light, we would not want to think of the surface as reflecting light differently. We could place a radiance meter at the point being illuminated to measure the light. However, for this to get an accurate reading

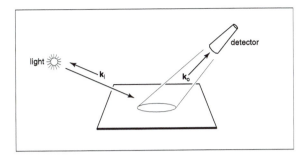

Figure 11.6. A simple measurement device for directional reflectance. The positions of light and detector are moved to each possible pair of directions.

that would not depend on the $\Delta\sigma$ of the detector, we would need the light to subtend a solid angle bigger than $\Delta\sigma$. Unfortunately, the measurement taken by our roving radiance detector in direction $\mathbf{k}_o$ will also count light that comes from points outside the new detector's cone. So this does not seem like a practical solution.

Alternatively, we can place an irradiance meter at the point on the surface being measured. This will take a reading that does not depend strongly on subtleties of the light source geometry. This suggests characterizing reflectance as a ratio:

$$\rho = \frac{L_s}{H}$$

where this fraction ρ will vary with incident and exitant directions $\mathbf{k}_i$ and $\mathbf{k}_o$, H is the irradiance for light position $\mathbf{k}_i$, and L_s is the surface radiance measured in direction $\mathbf{k}_o$. If we take such a measurement for all direction pairs, we end up with a 4D function $\rho(\mathbf{k}_i, \mathbf{k}_o)$. This function is called the *bidirectional reflectance distribution function* (BRDF). The BRDF is all we need to know to characterize the directional properties of how a surface reflects light.

11.6.1 Directional Hemispherical Reflectance

Given a BRDF it is straightforward to ask, "What fraction of incident light is reflected?" However, the answer is not so easy; the fraction reflected depends on the directional distribution of incoming light. For this reason we typically only set a fraction reflected for a fixed incident direction $\mathbf{k}_i$. This fraction is called the *directional hemispherical reflectance*. This fraction, $R(\mathbf{k}_i)$, is defined:

$$R(\mathbf{k}_i) = \frac{\text{power in all outgoing directions } \mathbf{k}_o}{\text{power in a beam from direction } \mathbf{k}_i}.$$

Note that this quantity is between zero and one for reasons of energy conservation. If we allow the incident Φ_i power to hit on a small area ΔA, then the irradiance is $\Phi_i/\Delta A$. Also, the ratio of the incoming power is just the ratio of the radiance exitance to irradiance:

$$R(\mathbf{k}_i) = \frac{E}{H}.$$

The radiance in a particular direction resulting from this power is by the definition of BRDF:

$$L(\mathbf{k}_o) = H\rho(\mathbf{k}_i, \mathbf{k}_o)$$
$$= \frac{\Phi_i}{\Delta A}.$$

And from the definition of radiance, we also have:

$$L(\mathbf{k}_o) = \frac{\Delta E}{\Delta \sigma_o \cos \theta_o}$$

where E is the radiant exitance of the small patch going in direction $\mathbf{k}_o$. Using these two definitions for radiance, we get:

$$H\rho(\mathbf{k}_i, \mathbf{k}_o) = \frac{\Delta E}{\Delta \sigma_o \cos \theta_o}.$$

Rearranging terms, we get:

$$\frac{\Delta E}{H} = \rho(\mathbf{k}_i, \mathbf{k}_o)\Delta \sigma_o \cos \theta_o.$$

This is just the small contribution to E/H that is reflected near the particular $\mathbf{k}_o$. To find the total $R(\mathbf{k}_i)$ we sum over all outgoing $\mathbf{k}_o$. In integral form, this is:

$$R(\mathbf{k}_i) = \int_{\text{all } \mathbf{k}_o} \rho(\mathbf{k}_i, \mathbf{k}_o) \cos \theta_o \, d\sigma_o.$$

11.6.2 Ideal Diffuse BRDF

An idealized diffuse surface is called *Lambertian*. Such surfaces are impossible in nature for thermodynamic reasons, but they do mathematically conserve energy. The Lambertian BRDF has ρ equal to a constant for all angles. This means the surface will have the same radiance for all viewing angles, and this radiance will be proportional to the irradiance.

If we compute $R(\mathbf{k}_i))$ for a Lambertian surface with $\rho = C$, we get:

$$
\begin{aligned}
R(\mathbf{k}_i) &= \int_{\text{all } \mathbf{k}_o} C \cos \theta_o \, d\sigma_o \\
&= \int_{\phi_o=0}^{2\pi} \int_{\theta_o=0}^{\pi} C \cos \theta_o \sin \theta_o \, d\theta_o \, d\phi_o \\
&= \pi C.
\end{aligned}
$$

Thus for a perfectly reflecting Lambertian surface ($R = 1$), we have $\rho = 1/\pi$ and for a Lambertian surface whose $R(\mathbf{k}_i) = r$, we have:

$$
\rho(\mathbf{k}_i, \mathbf{k}_o) = \frac{r}{\pi}.
$$

This is another example where the use of steradians for solid angles determines the normalizing constant and thus introduces factors of π.

11.7 TRANSPORT EQUATION

With the definition of BRDF, we can describe the radiance of a surface in terms of the incoming radiance from all different directions. Because in computer graphics we can use idealized mathematics that might be impractical to instantiate in the lab, we can also write the BRDF in terms of radiance only. If we take a small part of the light with solid angle $\Delta\sigma_i$ with radiance L_i, and "measure" the refected radiance in direction $\mathbf{k}_o$ due to this small piece of the light, we can compute a BRDF (Figure 11.7). The irradiance due to the small piece of light is $H = L_i \cos \theta_i \Delta\sigma_i$. Thus the BRDF is:

$$
\rho = \frac{L_o}{L_i \cos \theta_i \Delta\sigma_i}.
$$

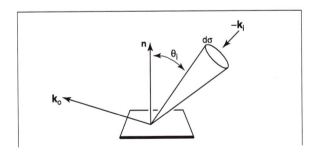

Figure 11.7. The geometry for the transport equation in its directional form.

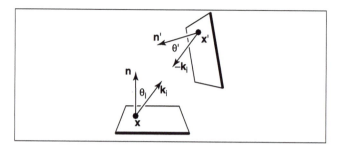

Figure 11.8. The light coming into one point comes from another point.

That form can be useful in some situations. Rearranging terms, we can write down the part of the radiance that is due to light coming from direction $\mathbf{k}_i$:

$$\Delta L_o = \rho(\mathbf{k}_i, \mathbf{k}_o) L_i \cos \theta_i \Delta \sigma_i.$$

If there is light coming from many directions $L_i(\mathbf{k}_i)$, we can sum all of them. In integral form, with notation for surface and field radiance, this is:

$$L_s(\mathbf{k}_o) = \int_{\text{all } \mathbf{k}_i} \rho(\mathbf{k}_i, \mathbf{k}_o) L_f(\mathbf{k}_i) \cos \theta_i d\sigma_i.$$

This equation is often called the *rendering equation* in computer graphics.

Sometimes it is useful to write the transport equation in terms of surface radiances only. Note that in a closed environment, the field radiance $L_f(\mathbf{k}_i)$ comes from some surface with surface radiance $L_s(-\mathbf{k}_i) = L_f(\mathbf{k}_i)$ (Figure 11.8). The solid angle subtended by the point $\mathbf{x}'$ in the figure is given by:

$$\Delta \sigma_i = \frac{\Delta A' \cos \theta'}{\|\mathbf{x} - \mathbf{x}'\|^2}$$

where $\Delta A'$ is the area we associate with $\mathbf{x}'$.

Substituting for $\Delta \sigma_i$ in terms of $\Delta A'$ suggests the following transport equation:

$$L_s(\mathbf{x}, \mathbf{k}_o) = \int_{\text{all } \mathbf{x}' \text{ visible to } \mathbf{x}} \frac{\rho(\mathbf{k}_i, \mathbf{k}_o) L_s(\mathbf{x}', \mathbf{x} - \mathbf{x}') \cos \theta_i \cos \theta' \, dA}{\|\mathbf{x} - \mathbf{x}'\|^2}.$$

Note that we are using a nonnormalized vector $\mathbf{x} - \mathbf{x}'$ to indicate the direction from $\mathbf{x}'$ to $\mathbf{x}$. Also note that we are writing L_s as a function of position and direction.

The only problem with this new transport equation is that the domain of integration is awkward. If we introduce a visibility function, we can trade off complexity in the domain with complexity in the integrand:

$$L_s(\mathbf{x}, \mathbf{k}_o) = \int_{\text{all } \mathbf{x}'} \frac{\rho(\mathbf{k}_i, \mathbf{k}_o) L_s(\mathbf{x}', \mathbf{x} - \mathbf{x}') v(\mathbf{x}, \mathbf{x}') \cos \theta_i \cos \theta' \, dA}{\|\mathbf{x} - \mathbf{x}'\|^2}$$

where

$$v(\mathbf{x}, \mathbf{x}') = \begin{cases} 1 & \text{if } \mathbf{x} \text{ and } \mathbf{x}' \text{ are mutually visible} \\ 0 & \text{otherwise.} \end{cases}$$

11.8 NOTES

A common radiometric quantity not described in this chapter is *radiant intensity* (I), which is the spectral power per steradian emitted from an infinitesimal point source. It should usually be avoided in graphics programs because point sources cause implementational problems. A more rigorous treatment of radiometry can be found in James Arvo's dissertation (Yale University, 1995). The radiometric and photometric terms in this chapter are from the *Illumination Engineering Society's* standard that is increasingly used by all fields of science and engineering.

12 | Path Tracing

This chapter describes *path tracing* where lighting is computed using Monte Carlo (MC) methods. Each ray in an MC method returns a noisy estimate, so many rays per pixel will be required. In the next chapter, we will add "shadow rays" to decrease the amount of noise.

12.1 LUMINAIRES

Before we can light anything, we need *luminaires*, which are light-emitting objects (lights). We will not have the directional or point sources used in many graphics programs. Instead, all of our luminaires will have an area, and light can be emitted or reflected from points on the surface of the luminaire. We find it convenient to decouple the directional distribution light emitted from a luminaire to the total power output from the luminaire. For a point $\mathbf{x}$ on the luminaire, we assume that radiant exitance (see Chapter 11) is described by a function $E(\mathbf{x})$. For a given point, we assume that the light emitted has a directional distribution $e(\mathbf{x}, \mathbf{k})$, which is a probability density function defined over outgoing directions $\mathbf{k}$. This is a restriction because it assumes the directional distribution is the same for all wavelengths. In practice, most luminaires do not violate that restriction. To render the luminaires, we need their radiance, which is given by

$$L(\mathbf{x}, \mathbf{k}) = \frac{E(\mathbf{x})e(\mathbf{x}, \mathbf{k})}{\mathbf{n} \cdot \mathbf{k}},$$

where $\mathbf{n}$ is the unit-length surface normal vector of the luminaire.

A simple and useful e is the phong density we saw in Chapter 10:

$$e(\mathbf{k}) = \frac{n+1}{2\pi}(\mathbf{n} \cdot \mathbf{k})^m,$$

where m is a control exponent. With $m = 1$, it is a diffuse luminiare whose

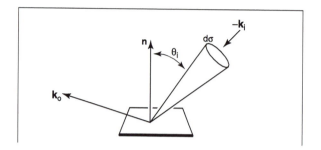

Figure 12.1. The geometry for the transport equation in its directional form.

radiance does not vary with **k**. With a large m, the light is concentrated near the surface normal vector **n**, as occurs with a car headlight.

12.2 MONTE CARLO SOLUTION TO LIGHT TRANSPORT

Recall that the main results of the last two chapters are the transport equation and Monte Carlo integration. The transport equation in directional form (Figure 12.1) is

$$L_s(\mathbf{k}_o) = \int_{\text{all } \mathbf{k}_i} \rho(\mathbf{k}_i, \mathbf{k}_o) L_f(\mathbf{k}_i) \cos \theta_i d\sigma_i. \tag{12.1}$$

Here, L_s the the surface (outgoing) radiance of the surface at a given point, and L_f is the field (incoming) radiance at the point. The Monte Carlo formula for one sample (Equation 10.5) is

$$\int_{x \in S} g(x) d\mu \approx \frac{g(x_0)}{p(x_0)}, \tag{12.2}$$

where x_0 is a random variable with underlying density p.

Because the transport equation is an integral, we can approximate it with Monte Carlo integration. Plugging Equation 12.1 into Equation 12.2 yields

$$L_s(\mathbf{k}_o) \approx \frac{\rho(\mathbf{k}_i, \mathbf{k}_o) L_f(\mathbf{k}_i) \cos \theta_i}{p(\mathbf{k}_i)}, \tag{12.3}$$

where vector $\mathbf{k}_i$ is chosen randomly with density p. This formula simplifies most when we use p to cancel out terms in the numerator, namely

$$p(\mathbf{k}_i) = \frac{\rho(\mathbf{k}_i, \mathbf{k}_o) \cos \theta_i}{R(\mathbf{k}_o)},$$

where R is the directional hemispherical reflectance. That particular choice of p yields

$$L_s(\mathbf{k}_o) \approx R(\mathbf{k}_o)L_f(\mathbf{k}_i). \tag{12.4}$$

Equation 12.4 has a particularly nice intuitive form; the radiance of a surface is just the fraction of energy reflected, multiplied by the color seen in the direction in which the viewing ray would scatter.

12.2.1 Lambertian Environments

To gain some intuition about applying Equation 12.4, assume that all reflective surfaces are Lambertian, i.e., R is a constant RGB color and $p(\mathbf{k}_i)$ is proportional to $\cos\theta_i$. Let's define a function *radiance* that returns the radiance seen along a ray:

RGB radiance(ray r)
if r hits at $\mathbf{x}$ **then**
    generate direction $\mathbf{b}$ with cosine density relative to the surface normal at $\mathbf{x}$
    ray $r_n = \mathbf{x} + t\mathbf{b}$
    return $L_e(\mathbf{x}) + R(\mathbf{p}) *$ radiance(r_n)
else
    return background(r).

Here, L_e is the emitted radiance, which is zero if $\mathbf{x}$ is not on a luminaire. This is a very easy function to write, but it will not terminate in enclosed environments without some maximum allowed depth. Note that a ray just keeps bouncing without branching (Figure 12.2). This is why it is called *path tracing*; a whole path is generated for each sample point on the screen. Note that for the particular ray shown in Figure 12.2 the estimate of radiance will be

$$L = L_{e1} + R_1(L_{e2} + R_2(L_{e3} + R_3 L_b)),$$

where R_i is the reflectance at $\mathbf{x}_i$; L_{ei} is the emitted radiance at $\mathbf{x}_i$; and L_b is the radiance of the background. Other rays through the same pixel will follow different random paths, and thus, will return different radiances. The average of all of these path values will be the pixel radiance.

The only missing detail is how one generates the random ray r_n with the right density. The cosine density is just the phong density (Equation 10.8) with $n = 1$:

$$p(\theta, \phi) = \frac{1}{\pi}\cos\theta.$$

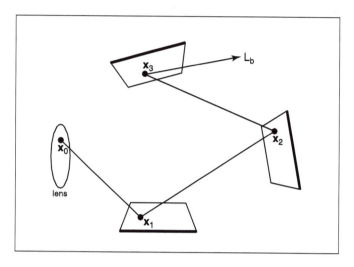

Figure 12.2. A single ray is sent from the lens in a diffuse path tracer bounces around the environment. It does not branch. It terminates when it misses all objects, or exceeds some maximum depth.

This implies

$$\cos\theta = \sqrt{1 - r_1},$$

$$\phi = 2\pi r_2,$$

where (r_1, r_2) are canonical random numbers (or better, one of the jittered samples for a ray). We can first convert the angles to a unit vector $\mathbf{b}$ with coordinates relative to the surface normal

$$\mathbf{b} = (\cos\phi\sin\theta, \sin\phi\sin\theta, \cos\theta).$$

Given an orthonormal basis *uvw* for the surface where $\mathbf{w}$ points in the direction of the outward surface normal, we can describe $\mathbf{b}$ in world coordinates:

$$\mathbf{b} = \cos\phi\sin\theta\mathbf{u} + \sin\phi\sin\theta\mathbf{v} + \cos\theta\mathbf{w}.$$

The $\sin\theta$ can be computed using $\sqrt{1 - \cos^2\theta}$.

A good way to initially debug this program is to use an enclosure of *any shape* with constant emitted radiance L_e and constant reflectance R. Your program should compute $L = E + RL_e + R^2 L_e + R^3 L_e \cdots$. The converged solution is

$$L = \frac{L_e}{1 - R}.$$

Try this with $R = L_e = 0.5$. Your program should have all pixels with value 1.0.

Figure 12.3. A 100 ray per pixel low-resolution path-traced image with a sphere of reflectance 1.0 and a luminaire with emitted radiance 1.0. This is a good debugging image because the color of the bottom sphere gradually increases as it nears the light source until it reaches that color at the point where they touch.

A more complicated example is the touching spheres, as shown in Figure 12.3. A "Cornell box" is shown in Figure 12.4. Note that this sort of path tracing is very noisy and thus requires many samples per pixel when there are small lights. We will address this problem by adding an explicit direct lighting algorithm in the next chapter.

Figure 12.4. A simple path traced image with 100 rays per pixel (left) and 1600 rays per pixel (right).

12.2.2   Specular Reflection

One nice thing about the path tracing from the last section is that we need not explicitly evaluate the BRDF ρ. Instead, we need to know the directional hemispherical reflectance $R(\theta)$ and have some way to generate random rays that reflect the same way light does from the surface. This is very easy for smooth metal mirrors, often called *specular* surfaces. Smooth metals obey two principles:

- *The law of reflection*, which states that the angle of incident light relative to the surface normal is the same as the angle of reflected light, and that the incident direction, surface normal, and reflected direction are coplanar.

- *The Fresnel equations*, which describe how much of the light is reflected, and by complement, how much is absorbed.

To implement the law of reflection, observe Figure 12.5, where the incident direction is $\mathbf{d}$, the surface normal vector is $\mathbf{n}$, and the reflected vector is $\mathbf{r}$. As can be seen in the figure, $\mathbf{r} = \mathbf{d} + 2\mathbf{a}$. The vector $\mathbf{a}$ is parallel to $\mathbf{n}$ but has length of $\mathbf{d}$ scaled by the cosine of the angle between $\mathbf{d}$ and $\mathbf{n}$. This yields

$$\mathbf{r} = \mathbf{d} + 2\mathbf{a} = \mathbf{d} - 2\frac{\mathbf{d} \cdot \mathbf{n}}{||\mathbf{n}||^2}\mathbf{n}.$$

Note that if $\mathbf{n}$ is a unit vector, dividing by the square of its length is not needed.

To compute the reflectance, the simplest approximation is to set it to some constant RGB value. This works well enough for most images. However, the reflectance of real metals increases as the angle between $\mathbf{d}$ and $\mathbf{n}$ increases. Schlick developed an accurate approximation to the rather ugly Fresnel equations

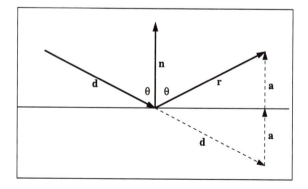

Figure 12.5. The reflection from a smooth surface.

to simulate the change in reflectance:

$$R(\theta) \approx R_0 + (1 - R_0)(1 - \cos\theta)^5, \tag{12.5}$$

where R_0 is the reflectance when $\mathbf{d}$ is parallel to $\mathbf{n}$. Try setting R_0 to 0.8 for all three channels RGB. This will make an object that behaves similarly to any modern "stainless" alloy. Although there is a small error implicit in Schlick's approximation, it is no bigger than the error we imposed when we decided not to use polarization, so you shouldn't worry about that.

12.2.3 Imperfect Specular Reflection

Often real specular surfaces slightly blur reflections due to irregularities on the surface that are on a fine scale. A classic example is the "back" side of aluminum foil. One way to simulate this is to add some noise to the specularly reflected ray. To do this we can use the same phong-like density we used to describe non-diffuse lights

$$p(\mathbf{k}) = \frac{n+1}{2\pi}(\mathbf{r} \cdot \mathbf{k})^m,$$

where $\mathbf{r}$ is the "ideally" reflected direction and $\mathbf{k}$ is the random direction. This assumes that $\mathbf{r}$ is a unit vector. For very large m this would look like a perfect mirror, and the reflections would become blurrier and blurrier as m gets smaller.

We can use the techniques of Chapter 10 to compute the random $\mathbf{k}$. Assuming that we are in a coordinate system where ϕ is an angle around $\mathbf{r}$, and (r_1, r_2) are a pair of canonical random numbers we have

$$(\mathbf{r} \cdot \mathbf{k}) = (1 - r_1)^{\frac{1}{n+1}}$$
$$\phi = 2\pi r_2.$$

If we build a uvw basis where $\mathbf{w} = \mathbf{r}$, this suggests we can create a $\mathbf{k}$ in global coordinates. One problem with this method is that $\mathbf{k}$ can be generated so that it is below the surface. This case can be detected by checking the sign of $\mathbf{k} \cdot \mathbf{n}$; when this is negative, either the radiance function can return zero, or a new ray can be generated with new random numbers until a ray above the surface is generated.

12.3 SMOOTH DIELECTRICS

A *dielectric* is a transparent material that refracts light. Diamonds, glass, water, and air are dielectrics. Dielectrics also filter light; some glass filters out more red and blue than green light, so the glass takes on a green tint. When a ray travels from a medium with refractive index n into one with a refractive index n_t, some of the light is transmitted, and it bends. This is shown for $n_t > n$ in Figure 12.6. Snell's law tells us that

$$n \sin \theta = n_t \sin \theta'.$$

From this and the equation $\sin^2 \theta + \cos^2 \theta = 1$, we can derive a relationship for cosines:

$$\cos^2 \theta' = 1 - \frac{n^2 \left(1 - \cos^2 \theta\right)}{n_t^2}.$$

From the figure, we can see that **n** and **b** form a basis for the plane of refraction.

Important note: the following discussion assumes **d** and **n** are unit vectors, so when you implement this, be sure to make unit length variables in this routine. By definition, we can describe **t** in this basis:

$$\mathbf{t} = \sin \theta' \mathbf{b} - \cos \theta' \mathbf{n}.$$

Since we can describe **d** in the same basis, and **d** is known, we can solve for **b**:

$$\begin{aligned} \mathbf{d} &= \sin \theta \mathbf{b} - \cos \theta \mathbf{n}, \\ \mathbf{b} &= \frac{\mathbf{d} + \mathbf{n} \cos \theta}{\sin \theta}. \end{aligned}$$

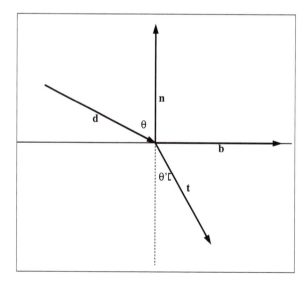

Figure 12.6. The refraction of light at a smooth surface.

This means we can solve for t with known variables:

$$\mathbf{t} = \frac{n \left(\mathbf{d} + \mathbf{n} \cos \theta \right)}{n_t} - \mathbf{n} \cos \theta \tag{12.6}$$

$$= \frac{n \left(\mathbf{d} - \mathbf{n}(\mathbf{d} \cdot \mathbf{n}) \right)}{n_t} - \mathbf{n} \sqrt{1 - \frac{n^2 \left(1 - (\mathbf{d} \cdot \mathbf{n})^2 \right)}{n_t^2}}. \tag{12.7}$$

Note that this equation works regardless of which of n and n_t is bigger. It is possible for there to be no real solution for $\cos \theta'$, which occurs when $\cos^2 \theta' < 0$. This will only occur for some angles and when $n_t < n$, and in that case, the number inside the *sqrt* above will be negative. In that case we have *total internal reflection*, where all of the light is reflected.

For the amount of light that is reflected and transmitted, we can still use Equation 12.5 for reflectance, being careful to use the larger of θ or θ'. The transmittance will be one minus the reflectance.

For homogeneous impurities as are found in typical glass, a light-carrying ray's intensity will be attenuated according to *Beer's Law*. As the ray travels through the medium, it loses intensity according to $dI = -CI\, dx$, where dx is distance. This means $dI/dx = -CI$. This is solved by the exponential $I = k \exp(-Cx)$. The strength of attenuation is described by the RGB attenuation constant a, which is the attenuation after one unit of distance. Putting in boundary conditions, we know that $I(0) = I_0$, and $I(1) = aI(0)$. The first implies $I(x) = I_0 \exp(-Cx)$. The second implies $I_0 a = I_0 \exp(-C)$ so $-C = \ln(a)$. So the final formula is

$$I(s) = I(0)e^{\ln(a)s},$$

where $I(s)$ is the intensity of the beam at distance s from the interface. In practice, we reverse-engineer a by eye because such data is rarely easy to find.

To add dielectric materials in our code, we need a way to determine when a ray is going "into" an object. The simplest way to do this is to assume that all objects are embedded in air with refractive index very close to 1.0, and that surface normals point "out" (toward the air). This concept is illustrated in Figure 12.7. We also need to either send two rays (reflected and transmitted), or we need to randomly choose which ray to send. To keep branching down, we advocate sending one ray. If the reflected ray is generated with probability P and the transmitted ray is sent with probability $1 - P$, then we need to weight them so we probabilistically get the full contribution, as shown here:

if we choose reflected ray **then**
    return $R(\theta)$ * radiance(reflected ray) $/P$
else
    return $(1 - R(\theta))$ * radiance(transmitted ray) / $(1 - P)$.

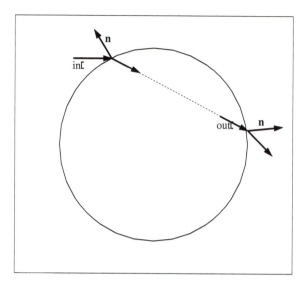

Figure 12.7. If a direction and the surface normal have a negative dot product, the direction points into the object. This is useful for deciding whether the ray bends in or out.

A conservative value for P is 0.5. In this case we effectively flip a coin to decide which ray, and multiply its color by two to account for the fact that we only choose it half the time. We could also let $P = R(\theta)$, but this is problematic when R is small and what it reflects is bright. A continuum between these extremes is

$$P = k/2 + (1 - k)R(\theta),$$

where k is chosen heuristically.

12.4 SPECULAR-DIFFUSE SURFACES

Many surfaces are dielectrics, but have small reflecting particles embedded which diffusely scatter light (e.g., plastic), or coat an underlying diffuse surface (e.g., finished wood). Such surfaces act as combinations of specular and diffuse surfaces. An interesting aspect of this behavior is that when the incoming light is "grazing" (θ is near 90 degrees), the specular component dominates, and when the incoming light is near-normal (θ is small), the diffuse interaction dominates. This is actually not surprising; the specular reflectance approximated by Equation 12.5 approaches one for the grazing case, so little light goes into the dielectric to interact with the subsurface material that creates the diffuse behavior. In the normal case, the typical normal reflectance is around five percent, so most of the light is transmitted to interact diffusely with the subsurface material.

Figure 12.8. The image on the left shows that we are randomly choosing wether to treat the surface as diffuse or specular. The two images on the right show that the image converges with more samples. These images also show the effect of varying reflectance with incident angle.

A simple model for these specular-diffuse surfaces just linearly combines specular and diffuse behavior. For the specular reflectance $R_s(\theta)$ we use Equation 12.5. Note that this is the same for all three RGB channels. For the diffuse reflectance we use $R_d(1 - R_s(\theta))$. Again, we can choose the specular ray with probability P and the diffuse ray with probability $1 - P$:

if we choose reflected ray **then**
    return $R(\theta)$ * radiance(reflected ray) $/P$
else
    return $(1 - R(\theta))$ * R_d * radiance(diffuse ray) / $(1 - P)$.

The spatial distributions of these rays can be chosen in the same way we chose rays for normal specular and Lambertian surfaces earlier in the chapter.

Note that we can either do direct lighting using the BRDF,

$$\rho = \frac{(1 - R(\theta))R_d}{\pi},$$

or we can do direct lighting only when we generate a diffusely scattered ray, i.e., with probability $1 - P$ which implies the BRDF:

$$\rho = \frac{(1 - R(\theta))R_d}{(1 - P)\pi}.$$

We use the latter method since, if anything, we oversample the direct lighting, so fewer shadow rays will speed things up without significantly affecting overall image quality.

12.5 IMAGE DISPLAY

A physically-based renderer can produce arbitrarily large RGB values to be displayed on a monitor or printed page. You will notice that to get surfaces with radiances in the $[0, 1]$ range you may need to have a luminaire whose radiances are much larger than 1. You will thus have reflections of luminaires that are too bright to display by mapping 1.0 to 255. You may also have a reasonable image, but all colors may be in the range $[0, 0.01]$ because of the units you choose. People use *tone mapping* to scale these quantities to a "reasonable" level that can be seen on the display. This is analogous to what photographers do to make sure their pictures are viewable. For example, a photo of a night scene is really much brighter than the night scene is.

The tone mapping problem was first defined by photographers; often, their goal is to produce realistic "renderings" of captured scenes, and they have to produce such renderings while facing the limitations presented by slides or prints on photographic papers. The challenges faced in tone reproduction for rendered or captured digital images are largely the same as those faced in conventional photography. The main difference is that digital images are in a sense "perfect" negatives, so no luminance information has been lost due to the limitations of the film process. This is a blessing in that detail is available in all luminance regions. We can apply a scaling that is analogous to setting exposure in a camera.

We first show how to set the tonal range of the output image based on the scene's key value. The key value is what we consider a "neutral" value in the image after display. For bright scenes like a snowy landscape, the key value will be above 0.5. For dark scenes, like mines, it will be below 0.1. For typical scenes something around 0.2 will work, with 0.18 being a commonly-used value. Like many tone reproduction methods, we view the log-average luminance as a useful approximation to the key of the scene. This quantity $\bar{L}_w$ is computed by

$$\bar{L}_w = \exp\left(\frac{1}{N}\sum_{x,y}\log\left(\delta + L_w(x, y)\right)\right),\tag{12.8}$$

where $L_w(x, y)$ is the "world" luminance for pixel (x, y); N is the total number of pixels in the image; and δ is a small value to avoid the singularity that occurs if black pixels are present in the image. For L_w, you can use the average of the RGB components, or another more sophisticated formula. If the scene has normal-key we would like to map this to the middle-grey of the displayed image, or 0.18 on a scale from zero to one. This suggests the equation

$$L(x, y) = \frac{a}{\bar{L}_w}L_w(x, y),\tag{12.9}$$

where $L(x, y)$ is a scaled luminance and $a = 0.18$. For low-key or high-key

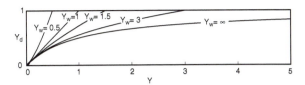

Figure 12.9. Display luminance as a function of world luminance for a family of values for Y_w.

images, a might vary from 0.18 up to 0.36 and 0.72 and vary it down to 0.09, and 0.045.

The main problem with Equation 12.9 is that many scenes have a predominantly normal dynamic range, but have a few high luminance regions near highlights or in the sky. In traditional photography this issue is dealt with by compression of both high and low luminances. However, modern photography has abandoned these "s"-shaped transfer curves in favor of curves that compress mainly the high luminances. A simple tone-mapping operator with these characteristics is given by

$$L_d(x,y) = \frac{L(x,y)}{1 + L(x,y)}, \qquad (12.10)$$

where L is that computed in Equation 12.9. Note that high luminances are scaled by approximately $1/L$, while low luminances are scaled by 1. The denominator causes a graceful blend between these two scalings. This formulation is guaranteed to bring all luminances within a displayable range. However, this is not always desirable because some burnout of highlights is visually acceptable and helps create a more usable range for medium-intensity pixels. Equation 12.10 can be extended to allow high luminances to burn out in a controllable fashion:

$$L_d(x,y) = \frac{L(x,y)\left(1 + \frac{L(x,y)}{L_{\text{white}}^2}\right)}{1 + L(x,y)}, \qquad (12.11)$$

where L_{white} is the smallest luminance that will be mapped to pure white. This function is a blend between Equation 12.10 and a linear mapping. It is shown for various values of L_{white} in Figure 12.9. If L_{white} value is set to the maximum luminance in the scene L_{max} or higher, no burn-out will occur. If it is set to infinity, then the function reverts to Equation 12.10. By default, we set L_{white} to the maximum luminance in the scene. If this default is applied to scenes that have a low dynamic range (i.e., $L_{\text{max}} < 1$), the effect is a subtle contrast enhancement.

12.6   C++ CODE

Below, we give a sample implementation of a material class. Our approach allows
a clean design in your ray tracer. A primitive now stores a pointer to a `Material`
and the `Material` has a pointer to a `Texture`. An intersected surface passes
a pointer to its material object back to the renderer, and the renderer queries it
directly. Note that we have added a function *seed* to the *Vector2* class, which
randomizes the vector in the range $[0, 1) \times [0, 1)$.

   The *Material::explicitBrdf* function will be used when we add direct lighting
in the next chapter.

The final iteration of our HitRecord yields the following:

```
struct SurfaceHitRecord
{
    float t;
    Vector3 p;          // point of intersection
    Vector3 texp;       // point of intersection for Texture mapping
    ONB uvw;            // w is the outward normal
    Vector2 uv;
    Material *mat_ptr;
};
```

12.6.1   Material Class

```
// Material.h

#ifndef _MATERIAL_H_
#define _MATERIAL_H_ 1


#include "Vector2.h"
#include "Ray.h"
#include "rgb.h"
#include "ONB.h"

class Material
{
public:
    virtual bool emits() const {return false;}

    virtual rgb emittedRadiance(const ONB&,      // ONB of hit point
            const Vector3&,                       // outgoing direction from light
            const Vector3&,                       // Texture point
            const Vector2&)                       // Texture coordinate
    { return rgb(0,0,0); }

    virtual rgb ambientResponse(const ONB&,      // ONB of hit point
            const Vector3&,                       // incident direction
            const Vector3&,                       // Texture point
            const Vector2& )                      // Texture coordinate
```

```
    { return rgb(0,0,0); }

    virtual bool explicitBrdf(const ONB&,        // ONB of hit point
        const Vector3&,                           // outgoing vector v0
        const Vector3&,                           // outgoing vector v1
        const Vector3&,                           // Texture point
        const Vector2&,                           // Texture coordinate
        rgb&) { return false; }

    virtual bool diffuseDirection( const ONB&,   // ONB of hit point
        const Vector3&,                           // incident vector
        const Vector3&,                           // Texture point
        const Vector2&,                           // Texture coordinate
        Vector2&,                                 // random seed
        rgb&,                                     // value returned by Texture
        Vector3&) { return false; }

    virtual bool specularDirection( const ONB&,  // ONB of hit point
        const Vector3&,                           // incident vector
        const Vector3&,                           // Texture point
        const Vector2&,                           // Texture coordinate
        Vector2&,                                 // random seed
        rgb&,                                     // value returned by Texture
        Vector3&) { return false; }

    virtual bool transmissionDirection( const ONB&, // ONB of hit point
        const Vector3&,                           // incident unit vector
        const Vector3&,                           // Texture point
        const Vector2&,                           // Texture coordinate
        const Vector2&,                           // random seed
        rgb&,                                     // extinction color
        float&,                                   // fresnel_scale
        Vector3&) { return false; }

    virtual bool isDiffuse() { return false; }
    virtual bool isSpecular() { return false; }
    virtual bool isTransmissive() { return false; }
    virtual int causticPhotons() { return 0; }
    virtual int globalPhotons() { return 0; }
    virtual rgb photonColor() { return rgb(0.0f, 0.0f, 0.0f); }
};

#endif // _MATERIAL_H_
```

12.6.2 Diffuse Material Class

```
// DiffuseMaterial.h

#ifndef _DIFFUSE_MATERIAL_H_
#define _DIFFUSE_MATERIAL_H_
```

```
#include "Material.h"

class Texture;

class DiffuseMaterial : public Material
{
public:
    DiffuseMaterial(Texture *t )
    { R = t; }
    virtual rgb ambientResponse(const ONB&,
            const Vector3&,     // incident direction
            const Vector3&,     // Texture point
            const Vector2& ) ;  // Texture coordinate

    virtual bool explicitBrdf(const ONB&,
            const Vector3&,     // unit vector v1
            const Vector3&,     // unit vector v0
            const Vector3&,     // Texture point
            const Vector2&,     // Texture coordinate
            rgb&) ;

    virtual bool diffuseDirection( const ONB&,
            const Vector3&,     // incident unit vector
            const Vector3&,     // Texture point
            const Vector2&,     // Texture coordinate
            Vector2&,           // random seed
            rgb&,
            Vector3&) ;

    Texture *R;
};

#endif // _DIFFUSE_MATERIAL_H_



// DiffuseMaterial.h

#include "DiffuseMaterial.h"
#include "Texture.h"

rgb DiffuseMaterial::ambientResponse(const ONB&, const Vector3&,
      const Vector3& p, const Vector2& uv)
{ return R->value(uv, p); }

bool DiffuseMaterial::explicitBrdf(const ONB&, const Vector3&,
      const Vector3&, const Vector3& p, const Vector2& uv, rgb& brdf)
{
    float k = .318309886184f; // 1.0 / M_PI
    brdf = k * R->value(uv, p);
    return true;
}
```

```
bool DiffuseMaterial::diffuseDirection( const ONB& uvw, const Vector3&,
       const Vector3& p, const Vector2& uv, Vector2& seed, rgb& color,
       Vector3& v_out)
{
    float pi = M_PI;
    float phi = 2 * pi * seed.x();
    float r = sqrt(seed.y());
    float x = r * cos(phi);
    float y = r * sin(phi);
    float z = sqrt(1 - x*x - y*y);

    color = R->value(uv, p);
    v_out = x*uvw.u() + y*uvw.v() + z*uvw.w();

    seed.scramble();
    return true;
}
```

12.6.3 Phong Metal Material Class

```
// PhongMetalMaterial.h

#ifndef _PHONG_METAL_MATERIAL_H_
#define _PHONG_METAL_MATERIAL_H_ 1

#include "Material.h"

class Texture;

class PhongMetalMaterial : public Material  {
public:

    PhongMetalMaterial(Texture *rt, Texture *et)
    { R = rt; phong_exp = et;}

    virtual rgb ambientResponse(const ONB&,
          const Vector3&,     // incident direction
          const Vector3&,     // Texture point
          const Vector2&);    // Texture coordinate

    virtual bool specularDirection( const ONB&,
          const Vector3&,     // incident unit vector
          const Vector3&,     // Texture point
          const Vector2&,     // Texture coordinate
          Vector2&,           // random seed
          rgb&,
          Vector3&);

    Texture *R;
    Texture *phong_exp;
```

```
};

#endif // _PHONG_METAL_MATERIAL_H_



// PhongMetalMaterial.cc

#include "PhongMetalMaterial.h"
#include "Texture.h"

rgb PhongMetalMaterial::ambientResponse(const ONB&, const Vector3&,
      const Vector3& p, const Vector2& uv)
{ return R->value(uv, p); }

bool PhongMetalMaterial::specularDirection(const ONB& uvw,
      const Vector3& v_in, const Vector3 p, const Vector2& uv,
      Vector2& seed, rgb& color, Vector3& v_out)
{
   float pi = M_PI;
   float phi = 2 * pi * seed.x();
   float exponent = phong_exp->value(uv, p).r();
   float cosTheta = pow(1-seed.y(),  1.0/(exponent+1));
   float sinTheta = sqrt(1 - cosTheta*cosTheta);
   float x = cos(phi) * sinTheta;
   float y = sin(phi) * sinTheta;
   float z = cosTheta;

   ONB basis;
   Vector3 w = v_in - 2*dot(v_in,uvw.w())*uvw.w();
   basis.initFromW( w );

   color = R->value(uv, p);
   v_out = x*basis.u() + y*basis.v() + z*basis.w();

   if (exponent < 10000) seed.scramble();
   return (dot(v_out, uvw.w()) > 0);
}
```

12.6.4 Diffuse-Specular Material Class

This class allows for arbitrary diffuse and specular material models.

```
// DiffSpecMaterial.h

#ifndef _DIFF_SPEC_MATERIAL_H_
#define _DIFF_SPEC_MATERIAL_H_ 1

#include <Material.h>
#include <RNG.h>

class DiffSpecMaterial : public Material
```

```
{
public:
   DiffSpecMaterial() {}
   DiffSpecMaterial(Material* d, Material* s, float r0=.05f)
   { diff_mat = d; spec_mat = s; R0 = r0; }

   virtual rgb ambientResponse(const ONB&,        // ONB of hit point
         const Vector3&,                          // incident direction
         const Vector3&,                          // Texture point
         const Vector2& );                        // Texture coordinate

   virtual bool explicitBrdf(const ONB&,          // ONB of hit point
         const Vector3&,                          // outgoing vector v0
         const Vector3&,                          // outgoing vector v1
         const Vector3&,                          // Texture point
         const Vector2&,                          // Texture coordinate
         rgb&);

   virtual bool scatterDirection(const Vector3&,// incident Vector
         const HitRecord&,                        // hit we are shading
         Vector2&,                                // random seed
         rgb&,                                    // color to attenuate by
         bool&,                                   // count emitted light?
         float&,                                  // brdf scale
         Vector3&);                               // scattered direction

   float R0;
   RNG rng;
   Material* diff_mat;
   Material* spec_mat;
};

#endif // _DIFF_SPEC_MATERIAL_H_

// DiffSpecMaterial.cc

#include "DiffSpecMaterial.h"

rgb DiffSpecMaterial::ambientResponse(const ONB& uvw, const Vector3& v_in,
      const Vector3& p, const Vector2& uv)
{
   float cosine = dot(v_in, uvw.w());
   if (cosine < 0.0f) cosine = -cosine;
   float temp1 = 1.0f - cosine;
   float R = R0 + (1.0f - R0) * temp1*temp1*temp1*temp1*temp1;
   float P = (R + 0.5f) / 2.0f;

   if (rng() <= P)
     return spec_mat->ambientResponse(uvw, v_in, p, uv);
   else
     return diff_mat->ambientResponse(uvw, v_in, p, uv);
}
```

```
bool DiffSpecMaterial::explicitBrdf(const ONB& uvw, const Vector3& v0,
        const Vector3& v1, const Vector3& p, const Vector2& uv, rgb& brdf)
{ return diff_mat->explicitBrdf(uvw, v0, v1, p, uv, brdf); }

bool DiffSpecMaterial::scatterDirection (const Vector3& v_in,
        const HitRecord& rec, Vector2& seed, rgb& color, bool& CEL,
        float& brdf, Vector3& v_out)
{
    float cosine = dot(v_in, rec.uvw.w());
    if (cosine < 0.0f) cosine = -cosine;
    float temp1 = 1.0f - cosine;
    float R = R0 + (1.0f - R0) * temp1*temp1*temp1*temp1*temp1;
    float P = (R + 0.5f) / 2.0f;

    // we assume that spec_mat and diff_mat return brdf_scales of 1
    if (rng() <= P)
    {
        brdf = R / P;
        return spec_mat->scatterDirection(v_in, rec, seed, color, CEL,
    temp1, v_out);
    }
    else
    {
        brdf = (1.0f - R) / (1.0f - P);
        return diff_mat->scatterDirection(v_in, rec, seed, color, CEL,
    temp1, v_out);
    }
}
```

12.6.5 Dielectric Material Class

This class assumes that the dielectric is surrounded by air with index of refraction approximated by 1. To support dielectrics within dielectrics, such as wine in a glass, you will need to store the index of refraction inside and outside the material. You can then use Equation 12.7.

```
// DielectricMaterial.h

#ifndef _DIELECTRIC_H_
#define _DIELECTRIC_H_ 1

#include "Material.h"
#include "rgb.h"
#include "Vector3.h"

class Texture;

class DielectricMaterial : public Material
{
public:
```

```
    DielectricMaterial() {}
    DielectricMaterial(float nt, const rgb& _ex);

    bool specularDirection( const ONB& uvw,
            const Vector3& in_dir,  // incident vector
            const Vector3& texp,    // Texture point
            const Vector2& uv,      // Texture coordinate
            Vector2& rseed,         // random seed
            rgb& ratio,
            Vector3& reflection);

    bool transmissionDirection( const ONB& uvw,
            const Vector3& in_dir,  // incident unit vector
            const Vector3& texp,    // Texture point
            const Vector2& uv,      // Texture coordinate
            const Vector2& rseed,   // random seed
            rgb& _extinction,
            float& fresnel_scale,
            Vector3& transmission);

    float R0;
    float nt;
    rgb   extinction;
};

#endif // _DIELECTRIC_H_



// DielectricMaterial.cc

#include "DielectricMaterial.h"
#include <math.h>

DielectricMaterial::DielectricMaterial(float _nt, const rgb& _ex)
    : nt(_nt), extinction(_ex)
{
    R0 = (nt - 1.0f) / (nt + 1.0f);
    R0 *= R0;

    float r = log(extinction.r());
    float g = log(extinction.g());
    float b = log(extinction.b());

    extinction = rgb(r, g, b);
}


bool DielectricMaterial::specularDirection( const ONB& uvw,
        const Vector3& in_dir,
        const Vector3& texp,
        const Vector2& uv,
        Vector2& rseed,
```

```
        rgb& ratio,
        Vector3& reflection)
{
    float scale;
    Vector3 normal = uvw.w();
    float cosine = dot(in_dir, normal);

    if (cosine < 0.0f)   // ray is incoming
    {
        reflection = reflect(in_dir, uvw.w());
        cosine = -cosine;

        // since assuming dielectrics are imbedded in air no need to
        // check for total internal reflection here
        float temp1 = 1.0f - cosine;
        scale = R0 + (1.0f - R0) * temp1*temp1*temp1*temp1*temp1;
    }
    else // (cosine > 0.0f) ray is outgoing
    {
        reflection = reflect(in_dir, -uvw.w());
        float temp2 = -(dot(in_dir, -normal));
        float root = 1.0f - (nt * nt) * (1.0f - temp2 * temp2);

        if (root < 0.0f) scale = 1.0f; // total internal reflection
        else
        {
            float temp3 = 1.0f - cosine;
            scale = R0 + (1.0f - R0) * temp3*temp3*temp3*temp3*temp3;
        }
    }
    // we pass back the ammount of reflected light
    ratio = rgb(scale, scale, scale);
    return true;
}


bool DielectricMaterial::transmissionDirection( const ONB& uvw,
        const Vector3& in_dir,
        const Vector3& texp,
        const Vector2& uv,
        const Vector2& rseed,
        rgb& _extinction,
        float& fresnel_scale,
        Vector3& transmission)
{
    Vector3 normal = uvw.w();
    float cosine = dot(in_dir, normal);

    if (cosine < 0.0f)   // ray is incoming
    {
        float temp1 = 1.0f / nt;
        cosine = -cosine;
        float root = 1.0f - (temp1 * temp1) * (1.0f - cosine * cosine);
```

```
        // since assuming dielectrics are imbedded in air no need to
        // check for total internal reflection here
        transmission = in_dir * temp1 + normal * (temp1* cosine - sqrt(root));

        _extinction = rgb(1.0f, 1.0f, 1.0f);
    }
    else // (cosine > 0.0f) ray is outgoing
    {
        float temp2 = (dot(in_dir, normal));
        float root = 1.0f - (nt * nt) * (1.0f - temp2 * temp2);

        if (root < 0.0f) return false; // total internal reflection
        else transmission = in_dir * nt + -normal * (nt * temp2 - sqrt(root));

        _extinction = extinction;
    }

    float temp3 = 1.0f - cosine;
    fresnel_scale = 1.0 - (R0 + (1.0f - R0) * temp3*temp3*temp3*temp3*temp3);
    return true;
}
```

12.7 NOTES

The roots of path tracing are in the original paper "An Improved Illumination Model for Shaded Display" (Whitted, *Communications of the ACM*, 1980). That work was expanded on to be more fully probabilistic in "Distributed Ray Tracing" (Cook, Porter, and Carpenter, *Computer Graphics (Proc. of SIGGRAPH '84)*, 1984). The modern version of path tracing was introduced in "The Rendering Equation" (Kajiya, *Computer Graphics (Proc. SIGGRAPH '86)*). The tone-mapping algorithm presented in this chapter is described in "Photographic Tone Reproduction for Digital Images" (Reinhard et al., *Transactions on Graphics* (Proc. SIGGRAPH '02), 2002).

13 | Explicit Direct Lighting

Recall Equation 12.4 from the last chapter,

$$L_s(\mathbf{k}_o) \approx R(\mathbf{k}_o)L_f(\mathbf{k}_i),$$

where $\mathbf{k}_i$ is a random direction that is consistent with the BRDF ρ. This ends up yielding noisy images because when $\mathbf{k}_i$ hits a luminaire it returns a very high value, and otherwise returns something near zero. The usual strategy to deal with this is to explicitly sample the luminaires for the "direct" lighting, that is light that arrives at the viewed surface directly from the luminaire.

If we did wish to compute the direct lighting from all surfaces, we could use the surface-based transport equation from Chapter 11 (Figure 13.1):

$$L_s(\mathbf{x}, \mathbf{k}_o) = \int_{\text{all } \mathbf{x}' \text{ on luminaires}} \frac{\rho(\mathbf{k}_i, \mathbf{k}_o)L_e(\mathbf{x}', \mathbf{x} - \mathbf{x}')v(\mathbf{x}, \mathbf{x}') \cos\theta_i \cos\theta' \, dA}{\|\mathbf{x} - \mathbf{x}'\|^2},$$

where L_e is the emitted radiance and

$$v(\mathbf{x}, \mathbf{x}') = \begin{cases} 1 & \text{if } \mathbf{x} \text{ and } \mathbf{x}' \text{ are mutually visible} \\ 0 & \text{otherwise.} \end{cases}$$

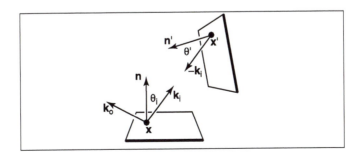

Figure 13.1. The configuration for the area-based transport equation.

Figure 13.2. A 100 sample rendering with simple path tracing (left) and shadow rays (right).

If we choose a random $\mathbf{x}'$ on a luminaire with underlying density $p(\mathbf{x}')$, the estimate for direct lighting is

$$L_s(\mathbf{x}, \mathbf{k}_o) \approx \frac{\rho(\mathbf{k}_i, \mathbf{k}_o) L_e(\mathbf{x}', \mathbf{x} - \mathbf{x}') v(\mathbf{x}, \mathbf{x}') \cos \theta_i \cos \theta'}{p(\mathbf{x}') \|\mathbf{x} - \mathbf{x}'\|^2}.$$

A p that will work is constant, that is, $p = 1/A$ where A is the area of the luminaire. This is a good choice for planar luminaires such as triangles.

In practice, a "shadow ray" is sent from $\mathbf{x}$ to $\mathbf{x}'$ to evaluate $v(\mathbf{x}, \mathbf{x}')$. This suggests the code

> *pick random point* $\mathbf{x}'$ *with density* p *on luminaire*
> $\mathbf{d} = (\mathbf{x}' - \mathbf{x})$
> *if ray* $\mathbf{x} + t\mathbf{d}$ *hits at* $\mathbf{x}'$ *then*
>   *return* $\rho(\mathbf{k}_i, \mathbf{k}_o) L_e(\mathbf{x}') (\mathbf{n} \cdot \mathbf{d}) (-\mathbf{n}' \cdot \mathbf{d}) / p(\mathbf{x})' \|\mathbf{d}\|^4$
> *else*
>   *return 0.*

The above code needs some extra tests such as clamping the cosines to zero if they are negative. Note that the term $\|\mathbf{d}\|^4$ comes from the distance squared term and the two cosines, e.g., $\mathbf{n} \cdot \mathbf{d} = \|\mathbf{d}\| \cos \theta$ because $\mathbf{d}$ is not necessarily a unit vector. The difference between using shadow rays and not using them for a 100 sample image is shown in Figure 13.2. A more complex scene is shown in Figure 13.3. Several examples of soft shadows are shown in Figure 13.4.

Figure 13.3. An image computed using a path tracer with shadow rays. The gloss on the tables uses the diffuse-specular model from the last chapter.

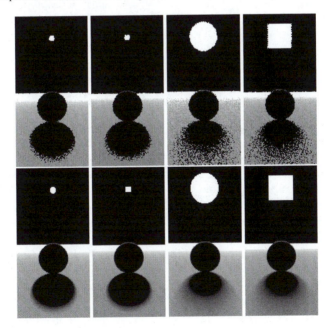

Figure 13.4. Various soft shadows on a backlit sphere with a square and a spherical light source. Top: one sample. Bottom: 100 samples. Note that the shape of the light source is less important than its size in determining shadow appearance.

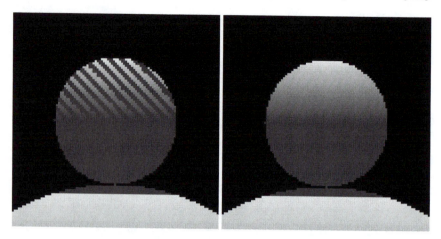

Figure 13.5. Left: Using an interval $t \in (0, \infty)$ causes some rays to hit the surface at **q**, causing black pixels. Right: Using $t \in (\epsilon, \infty)$ avoids these artifacts.

A problem to keep in mind is that because of finite-precision aritmetic, the shadow ray may intersect the surface **q** at some t value other than zero. If this number is positive, we will detect a false shadow as shown in Figure 13.5 (left).

Sometimes these dark pixels are more irregular and resemble a Moiré pattern. Instead, we pick some small ϵ that t must be bigger than. This is an inelegant hack, but it usually solves the problem.

13.1 DIRECT LIGHTING IN A PATH TRACER

The path-tracing program in the last chapter sent random rays that queried the total radiance in various directions. If we compute the direct light at **x** then we are double counting if we let a scattered ray originating at **x** "see" the emitted light if it happens to hit a luminaire. So the function *radiance* should be replaced with *reflected radiance*. However, there is a big problem with this: mirrors behave poorly when you use explicit direct lighting on them. The reason for this is that for a mirror, the BRDF ρ is very narrow, and the variance of direct lighting will be very high. So for specular surfaces we do want to use the method from the last chapter with no shadow rays.

In practice, it is simplest to have one *radiance* function that returns the radiance seen in a direction, but add a boolean variable *count emitted light* (CEL) to the argument list that signals whether to add the emitted component when a luminaire is hit. This idea is shown in Figure 13.6

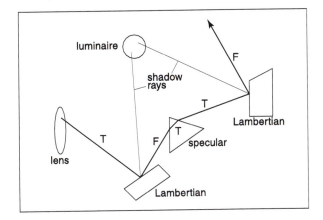

Figure 13.6. For a path through the environment, each of the segments either "sees" emitted light (CEL = T) or it does not (CEL = F). If the previous surface sent a shadow ray so already counted emitted light, the segment does not see emitted light.

13.2 SAMPLING A SPHERICAL LUMINAIRE

Although a sphere with center $\mathbf{c}$ and radius r can be sampled using uniform random points on the luminaire, this will yield a very noisy image because many samples will be on the back of the sphere, and the $\cos \theta'$ term varies so much. Instead, we can use a more complex $p(\mathbf{x}')$ to reduce noise. The first nonuniform density we might try is $p(\mathbf{x}') \propto \cos \theta'$. This turns out to be just as complicated as sampling with $p(\mathbf{x}') \propto \cos \theta' / \|\mathbf{x}' - \mathbf{x}\|^2$, so we instead discuss that here. We observe that sampling on the luminaire this way is the same as using a density constant function $q(\mathbf{k}_i) = \text{const}$ defined in the space of directions subtended by the luminaire as seen from $\mathbf{x}$. We now use a coordinate system defined with $\mathbf{x}$ at the origin, and a right-handed orthonormal basis with (see Figure 13.7)

$$\mathbf{w} = \frac{\mathbf{c} - \mathbf{x}}{\|\mathbf{c} - \mathbf{x}\|}.$$

We also define (α, ϕ) to be the azimuthal and polar angles with respect to the uvw coordinate system.

The maximum α that includes the spherical luminaire is given by

$$\alpha_{\max} = \arcsin\left(\frac{r}{\|\mathbf{x} - \mathbf{c}\|}\right) = \arccos \sqrt{1 - \left(\frac{r}{\|\mathbf{x} - \mathbf{c}\|}\right)^2}.$$

Thus, a uniform density (with respect to solid angle) within the cone of directions subtended by the sphere is just the reciprocal of the solid angle subtended by the

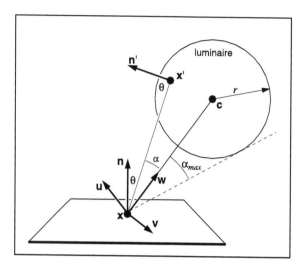

Figure 13.7. Geometry for spherical luminaire.

sphere

$$q(\mathbf{k}_i) = \frac{1}{2\pi(1 - \cos \alpha_{\max})},$$

and we get

$$\begin{bmatrix} \cos \alpha \\ \phi \end{bmatrix} = \begin{bmatrix} 1 + \xi_1(\cos \alpha_{\max} - 1) \\ 2\pi\xi_2 \end{bmatrix}.$$

This gives us the direction to $\mathbf{x}'$. To find the actual point, we need to find the first point on the sphere in that direction. The ray in that direction is just $(\mathbf{x} + t\mathbf{a})$, where $\mathbf{a}$ is given by

$$\mathbf{a} = \mathbf{u} \cos \phi \sin \alpha + \mathbf{v} \sin \phi \sin \alpha + \mathbf{w} \cos \alpha.$$

We must also calculate $p(\mathbf{x}')$, the probability density function with respect to the area measure (recall that the density function q is defined in solid angle space). Since we know that q is a valid probability density function using the σ measure, and we know that

$$d\sigma(\mathbf{k}_i) = \frac{dA(\mathbf{x}') \cos \theta'}{\|\mathbf{x} - \mathbf{x}'\|^2},$$

we can relate any probability density function $q(\mathbf{k}_i)$ with its associated probability density function $p(\mathbf{x}')$ for the region defined by dA and the corresponding $d\sigma$ (Figure 13.9):

$$q(\mathbf{k}_i)d\sigma(\mathbf{k}_i) = p(\mathbf{x}')dA(\mathbf{x}').$$

Figure 13.8. A sphere with $L_e = 1$ touching a sphere of reflectance 1; The reflective sphere should have $L(\mathbf{x}) = 1$ where they touch. Left: one sample. Middle: 100 samples. Right: 100 samples, close-up.

This allows us to convert between q and p:

$$p(\mathbf{x}') = \frac{q(\mathbf{k}_i) \cos \theta'}{\|\mathbf{x} - \mathbf{x}'\|^2}. \tag{13.1}$$

A good debugging case for this is shown in Figure 13.8.

13.3 DIRECT LIGHTING FROM MANY LUMINAIRES

Traditionally, when N_L luminaires are in a scene, the direct lighting integral is broken into N_L separate integrals. This implies that at least N_L samples must be taken to approximate the direct lighting, or, some bias must be introduced. This is what you should probably do when you first implement your program. However, you can later leave the direct lighting integral intact and design a probability density function over all N_L luminaires.

As an example, suppose we have two luminaires, l_1 and l_2, and we devise two probability functions, $p_1(\mathbf{x}')$ and $p_2(\mathbf{x}')$, where $p_i(\mathbf{x}') = 0$ for $\mathbf{x}'$ not on l_i and $p_i(\mathbf{x}')$ is found by a method such as one of those described previously for generating $\mathbf{x}'$ on l_i. These functions can be combined into a single density over both lights by applying a weighted average

$$p(\mathbf{x}') = \alpha p_1(\mathbf{x}') + (1 - \alpha) p_2(\mathbf{x}'),$$

where $\alpha \in (0, 1)$. We can see that p is a probability density function because its integral over the two luminaires is one, and it is strictly positive at all points on the luminaires. Densities that are "mixed" from other densities are often called *mixture densities*, and the coefficients α and $(1-\alpha)$ are called the *mixing weights*.

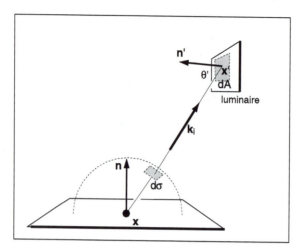

Figure 13.9. Integrating over the luminaire. Note that there is a direct correspondence between dA, the differential area on the luminaire, and $d\sigma$, the area of the projection of dA onto the unit sphere centered at **x**.

To estimate $L = (L_1 + L_2)$, where L is the direct lighting and L_i is the lighting from luminaire l_i, we first choose a random canonical pair (ξ_1, ξ_2), and use it to decide which luminaire will be sampled. If $0 \le \xi_1 < \alpha$, we estimate L_1 with e_1 using the methods described previously to choose **x'** and to evaluate $p_1(\mathbf{x'})$, and we estimate L with e_1/α. If $\xi_1 \ge \alpha$, then we estimate L with $e_2/(1-\alpha)$. In either case, once we decide which source to sample, we cannot use (ξ_1, ξ_2) directly because we have used some knowledge of ξ_1. So, if we choose l_1 (so $\xi_1 < \alpha$), then we choose a point on l_1 using the random pair $(\xi_1/\alpha, \xi_2)$. If we sample l_2 (so $\xi_1 \ge \alpha$), then we use the pair $((\xi_1 - \alpha)/(1 - \alpha), \xi_2)$. This way, a collection of stratified samples will remain stratified in some sense. Note that it is to our advantage to have ξ_1 stratified in one dimension, as well as having the pair (ξ_1, ξ_2) stratified in two dimensions, so that the l_i we choose will be stratified over many (ξ_1, ξ_2) pairs, so some multijittered sampling method may be helpful.

This basic idea used to estimate $L = (L_1 + L_2)$ can be extended to N_L luminaires by mixing N_L densities

$$p(\mathbf{x'}) = \alpha_1 p_1(\mathbf{x'}) + \alpha_2 p_2(\mathbf{x'}) + \cdots + \alpha_{N_L} p_{N_L}(\mathbf{x'}), \qquad (13.2)$$

where the α_is sum to 1, and where each α_i is positive if l_i contributes to the direct lighting. The value of α_i is the probability of selecting a point on the l_i, and p_i is then used to determine which point on l_i is chosen. If l_i is chosen, then we estimate L with e_i/α_i. Given a pair (ξ_1, ξ_2), we choose l_i by enforcing the

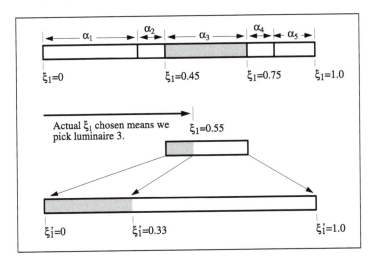

Figure 13.10. Diagram of mapping ξ_1 to choose l_i and the resulting remapping to new canonical sample ξ_1'.

conditions

$$\sum_{j=1}^{i-1} \alpha_j < \xi_1 < \sum_{j=1}^{i} \alpha_j.$$

And to sample the light, we can use the pair (ξ_1', ξ_2), where

$$\xi_1' = \frac{\xi_1 - \sum_{j=1}^{i-1} \alpha_j}{\alpha_i}.$$

This basic process is shown in Figure 13.10. It cannot be overstressed that it is important to "reuse" the random samples in this way to keep the variance low, in the same way we used stratified sampling (jittering) instead of random sampling in the space of the pixel. To choose the point on the luminaire l_i given (ξ_1', ξ_2), we can use the same types of p_i for luminaires as used in the last section. The question remaining is what to use for α_i.

13.3.1 Choosing the Weights

The simplest way to choose values for α_i is to choose values where all weights are made equal: $\alpha_i = 1/N_L$ for all i. This would definitely make a valid estimator because the α_i sum to 1, and none of them is zero. Unfortunately, in many scenes this estimate would produce a high variance (when the L_i are very different, as occurs in most night "walkthroughs"), but it is useful for debugging.

Suppose we had perfect p_i defined for all the luminaires. A zero-variance solution would then result if we could set $\alpha_i \propto L_i$, where L_i is the contribution from the ith luminaire. If we can make α_i approximately proportional to L_i, then we should have a fairly good estimator. We call this the *linear method* of setting α_i, because the time used to choose one sample is linearly proportional to N_L, the number of luminaires.

To obtain such α_i, we get an estimated contribution e_i at $\mathbf{x}$ by approximating the rendering equation for l_i with the geometry term set to one. These e_is (from all luminaires) can be directly converted to α_i by scaling them so their sum is 1:

$$\alpha_i = \frac{e_i}{e_1 + e_2 + \cdots + e_{N_L}}. \tag{13.3}$$

This method of choosing α_i will be valid because all potentially visible luminaires will end up with positive α_i. We should expect the highest variance in areas where shadowing occurs, because this is where setting the geometry term to 1 causes α_i to be a poor estimate.

Implementing the linear α_i method has several subtleties. If the entire luminaire is below the tangent plane at $\mathbf{x}$, then the estimate for e_i should be zero. An easy mistake to make is to set e_i to zero if the center of the luminaire is below the horizon. This will make α_i take the one value that is not allowed: an incorrect zero. Such a bug will become obvious in pictures of spheres illuminated by luminaires that subtend large solid angles, but for many scenes, such errors are not noticeable. To overcome this problem, we make sure that for a polygonal luminaire, all of its vertices are below the horizon before it is given a zero probability of being sampled. For spherical luminaires, we check that the center of the luminaire is a distance greater than the sphere radius under the horizon plane before it is given a zero probability of being sampled.

13.4 C++ CODE

13.4.1 Parallelogram Class

Parallelograms are very useful as light sources. This implementation shows the final form of the Shape class, complete with a *randomPoint* funcion.

```
// Parallelogram.h

#ifndef _PARALLELOGRAM_H_
#define _PARALLELOGRAM_H_ 1

#include "Shape.h"
#include "Material.h"
```

```
#include "BBox.h"

#define PARALLEL_EPSILON 0.00000001f

class Parallelogram : public Shape
{
public:
    Parallelogram(const Vector3& _base, const Vector3& _u, const Vector3& _v,
        Material* _mptr);

    Parallelogram(const Vector3& _base, const Vector3& _u, const Vector3& _v,
        const Vector2& _uv0, const Vector2& _uv1, const Vector2& _uv2,
        Material* _mptr);

    bool hit(const Ray& r, float tmin, float tmax, float time,
        HitRecord& rec) const;

    bool shadowHit(const Ray& r, float tmin, float tmax, float time)const;

    BBox boundingBox(float time0, float time1) const;

    bool randomPoint(const Vector3& viewpoint, const Vector2& seed , float time,
        Vector3& light_point, Vector3& N,
        float& pdf, rgb& radiance) const;

    Vector3 base;  //
    Vector3 u;     //  One vertex and the offsets to its neighbors
    Vector3 v;     //

    Vector3 norm;  // normal of the parallelogram
    Vector3 unorm; // normalized u offset
    Vector3 vnorm; // normalized v offset

    Vector2 uv0;   //
    Vector2 uv1;   // texture coords
    Vector2 uv2;   //

    float _pdf;    // precomputed constant pdf
    Material* mptr;
};

#endif //_PARALLELOGRAM_H_

// Parallelogram.cc

#include "Parallelogram.h"

Parallelogram::Parallelogram(const Vector3& _base, const Vector3& _u,
                             const Vector3& _v, Material* _mptr)
    : base(_base), u(_u), v(_v)
{
    mptr = _mptr;
    norm = unitVector(cross(u,v));
```

```
      unorm = unitVector(u);
      vnorm = unitVector(v);

      uv0 = Vector2(0, 0);
      uv1 = Vector2(1, 0);
      uv2 = Vector2(0, 1);
      // find area of parallelogram
      double width  = u.length();
      Vector3 proj  = v - ((dot(v, u) / (width*width)) * u);
      double height = proj.length();
      double area   = width * height;

      _pdf = 1.0f / area;
}

Parallelogram::Parallelogram(const Vector3& _base, const Vector3& _u,
      const Vector3& _v, const Vector2& _uv1,
      const Vector2& _uv2, Material* _mptr)
: base(_base), u(_u), v(_v), uv0(_uv0), uv1(_uv1), uv2(_uv2)
{
   mptr = _mptr;
   norm  = unitVector(cross(u,v));
   unorm = unitVector(u);
   vnorm = unitVector(v);

   // find area of parallelogram
   double width  = u.length();
   Vector3 proj = v - ((dot(v, u) / (width*width)) * u);
   double height = proj.length();
   double area   = width * height;

   _pdf = 1.0f / area;
}

bool Parallelogram::hit(const Ray& r, float tmin, float tmax, float time,
      HitRecord& rec) const
{
   double dot1 = dot(r.direction(), norm);

   // check to see if ray is parallel to surface plane
   if (dot1 < PARALLEL_EPSILON && dot1 > -PARALLEL_EPSILON) return false;

   // find distance to surface plane
   float dot2 = dot(norm, base);
   float t    = (dot2 - dot(norm, r.origin())) / dot1;
   if (t > tmax || t < tmin) return false;

   // see if point of plane intersection is within parallelogram
   Vector3 hit_plane(r.origin() + r.direction() * t);
   Vector3 offset(hit_plane - base);

   float u1 = dot(unorm, offset) / u.length();
   if (u1 < 0.0f || u1 > 1.0f) return false;
```

```
        float v1 = dot(vnorm, offset) / v.length();
    if (v1 < 0.0f || v1 > 1.0f) return false;


    // fill hit record
    rec.mat_ptr = mptr;
    rec.p = rec.texp = hit_plane;
    rec.t = t;

    rec.uvw.initFromW(norm);
    rec.uv = v1 * uv2 + (1.0f - v1) * uv0 + u1 * uv1;
    return true;
}

bool Parallelogram::shadowHit(const Ray& r, float tmin, float tmax,
        float time)const
{
    double dot1 = dot(r.direction(), norm);

    // check to see if ray is parallel to surface plane
    if (dot1 < PARALLEL_EPSILON && dot1 > -PARALLEL_EPSILON) return false;

    // find distance to surface plane
    float dot2 = dot(norm, base);
    float t    = (dot2 - dot(norm, r.origin())) / dot1;
    if (t > tmax || t < tmin) return false;

    // see if point of plane intersection is within parallelogram
    Vector3 hit_plane(r.origin() + r.direction() * t);
    Vector3 offset(hit_plane - base);

    float u1 = dot(unorm, offset) / u.length();
    if (u1 < 0.0f || u1 > 1.0f) return false;

    float v1 = dot(vnorm, offset) / v.length();
    return (v1 >= 0.0f || v1 <= 1.0f) ;
}

BBox Parallelogram::boundingBox(float time0, float time1) const
{
    const float epsilon = 0.00001f;

    Vector3 min;
    Vector3 max;

    Vector3 p0 = base;
    Vector3 p1 = base + u;
    Vector3 p2 = base + v;
    Vector3 p3 = base + u + v;

    min.setX(p0.x() < p1.x() ? p0.x() : p1.x());
    min.setY(p0.y() < p1.y() ? p0.y() : p1.y());
    min.setZ(p0.z() < p1.z() ? p0.z() : p1.z());
```

```
    min.setX(p2.x() < min.x() ? p2.x() : min.x());
    min.setY(p2.y() < min.y() ? p2.y() : min.y());
    min.setZ(p2.z() < min.z() ? p2.z() : min.z());

    min.setX(p3.x() < min.x() ? p3.x() : min.x());
    min.setY(p3.y() < min.y() ? p3.y() : min.y());
    min.setZ(p3.z() < min.z() ? p3.z() : min.z());

    max.setX(p0.x() > p1.x() ? p0.x() : p1.x());
    max.setY(p0.y() > p1.y() ? p0.y() : p1.y());
    max.setZ(p0.z() > p1.z() ? p0.z() : p1.z());

    max.setX(p2.x() > max.x() ? p2.x() : max.x());
    max.setY(p2.y() > max.y() ? p2.y() : max.y());
    max.setZ(p2.z() > max.z() ? p2.z() : max.z());

    max.setX(p3.x() > max.x() ? p3.x() : max.x());
    max.setY(p3.y() > max.y() ? p3.y() : max.y());
    max.setZ(p3.z() > max.z() ? p3.z() : max.z());

    min.setX(min.x() - epsilon);
    min.setY(min.y() - epsilon);
    min.setZ(min.z() - epsilon);

    max.setX(max.x() + epsilon);
    max.setY(max.y() + epsilon);
    max.setZ(max.z() + epsilon);

    return BBox(min, max);
}

bool Parallelogram::randomPoint(const Vector3& viewpoint, const Vector2& seed,
        float time, Vector3& light_point, Vector3& N, float & pdf,
        rgb& radiance) const
{
    light_point = Vector3(base + seed.x() * u + seed.y() * v);
    pdf = _pdf;

    Vector3 from_light = unitVector(viewpoint - light_point);
    ONB uvw;
    uvw.initFromW(norm);
    N = uvw.w();

    radiance = mptr->emittedRadiance(uvw, from_light, light_point,
                                Vector2(0.0f,0.0f));

    return true;
}
```

13.4.2 Random Point Functions

Here we give *randomPoint* functions for use in your existing sphere and triangle classes.

```cpp
bool Sphere::randomPoint(const Vector3& viewpoint, const Vector2& seed,
        float time, Vector3& on_light, Vector3& N, float& pdf, rgb& E)const
{
    float d = (viewpoint - center).length();
    if (d < radius) return false;
    float r = radius;
    float pi = M_PI;

    // internal angle of cone surrounding light seen from viewpoint
    float sin_alpha_max = r / d;
    float cos_alpha_max = sqrt(1 - sin_alpha_max*sin_alpha_max);
    float q = 1. / (2*pi*(1- cos_alpha_max));

    float cos_alpha = 1 + seed.x()*(cos_alpha_max-1);
    float sin_alpha = sqrt(1 - cos_alpha*cos_alpha);

    float phi = 2 * pi * seed.y();
    float cos_phi = cos(phi);
    float sin_phi = sin(phi);

    Vector3 k_i(cos_phi * sin_alpha, sin_phi * sin_alpha, cos_alpha);

    // Construct the local coordinate system UVW where viewpoint is at
    // the origin and the Sphere is at (0,0,d) in UVW.
    ONB UVW;
    UVW.initFromW(center - viewpoint);
    Ray to_light(viewpoint,
  k_i.x() * UVW.u() + k_i.y() * UVW.v() + k_i.z() * UVW.w());



    SurfaceHitRecord rec;
    if (this->hit(to_light, 0.00001, FLT_MAX, time, rec)) {
        on_light = rec.p;
        float cos_theta_prime = -dot(rec.uvw.w(), to_light.direction());
        pdf = q * cos_theta_prime / ( on_light - viewpoint ).squaredLength();
        N = rec.uvw.w();
        E = mat_ptr->emittedRadiance( rec.uvw, -to_light.direction(),
      on_light, rec.uv );
        return true;
    }
    else
        return false;
}
```

```
bool Triangle::randomPoint(const Vector3& viewpoint, const Vector2& seed,
        float time, Vector3& light_point, Vector3& N, float& pdf,
        rgb& radiance)const
{
    float temp  = sqrt(1.0f - seed.x());
    float beta  = (1.0f - temp);
    float gamma = temp*seed.y();
    light_point = (1.0f - beta - gamma)*p0 + beta*p1 + gamma*p2;

    Vector3 from_light = unitVector(viewpoint - light_point);
    ONB uvw;
    N = unitVector(cross((p1 - p0), (p2 - p0)));
    uvw.initFromW(N);

    radiance = mptr->emittedRadiance(uvw, from_light, light_point,
    Vector2(0.0f,0.0f));

    return true;

}
```

13.5   NOTES

Probabilistic direct lighting was introduced in "Distributed Ray Tracing" (Cook, Porter, and Carpenter, *Computer Graphics (Proc. SIGGRAPH '84)*, 1984). For models with many many lights, a more sophisticated startegy for choosing lights is needed as discussed in "Monte Carlo Techniques for Direct Lighting Calculations" (Shirley, Wang, and Zimmerman, *ACM Transactions on Graphics*, 1996). An elegant discussion of how to best apply direct lighting for general BRDFs is given in "Optimally Combining Sampling Techniques for Monte Carlo Rendering" (Veach and Guibas, *Proceedings of SIGGRAPH 95, Computer Graphics Proceedings, Annual Conference Series*, 1995).

14 | Photon Mapping

The biggest problem with path tracing is that it is far too noisy when there are specular surfaces and luminaires that are not large in area. This is because shadow rays reduce noise only for light that comes directly from luminaire to a surface. Light that goes from luminaire to mirror to diffuse surface will create a noisy reflected pattern. The most popular way to solve this problem is to supplement a path tracer with *photon mapping*. This method sends out energy packets from the luminaires and marks the scene with them. Where there are many photons, it is bright. It will turn out that we need too many photons if we try to do all lighting this way, but using photons after the first reflection turns out to be a very effective way to help a path tracer work well.

14.1 SENDING PHOTONS

Before we can take advantage of photons, we need to propagate them and store them in the environment. First, note that in the rendering literature, one of these "photons" is really an energy packet with many wavelentgths mixed together. The jth photon will have a color $\Delta\Phi_j$. When a photon hits a surface we store its power, its 3D position $\mathbf{x}_j$, and its incident direction. We could instead store the power after the photon interacts with a surface but it is better to store information about incident photons for reasons discussed below. For each luminaire we figure out the total emitted power Φ and send m photons each with power Φ/m. The for each photon a random direction is chosen with a directional distribution appropriate for the luminaire. Then we follow a simple algorithm:

> done = false
> select emitted ray e
> $\Delta\Phi = \Phi/m$
> **while** not done **do**
>   **if** e hits at $\mathbf{x}$ **then**
>   if $\mathbf{x}$ is not specular store $(Delta\Phi, e.\text{direction}, \mathbf{x})$ in photon map

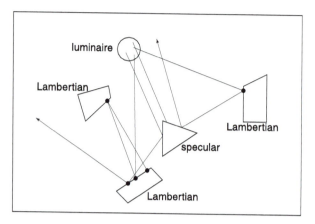

Figure 14.1. Photons are stored when they hit non-specular surfaces. At each interaction they may be absorbed or scattered.

R = directional hemispherical reflectance at $\mathbf{x}$ for e
if random $s <$ average(R) **then**
    scatter e in random direction with origin $\mathbf{x}$
    $\Delta\Phi = (R/s) * \Delta\Phi$
else
    done = true
else
    done = true

Here s is a uniform random variable in $[0, 1)$ and the random direction is computed the same way as for viewing rays in Chapter 12. The photon tracing process is shown in Figure 14.1.

Photons should be stored in a data structure over space rather than surfaces. This way no assumptions about surface types is needed, and the clean interface of ray tracing can be preserved.

14.2 USING THE PHOTON MAP

When a viewing ray hits a specular surface we proceed as before. If we hit a non-specular surface at point $\mathbf{x}$ we look at all photons within a radius r of $\mathbf{x}$ to get an estimate of the radiance seen at $\mathbf{x}$ (Figure 14.2). This will cause some blurring aoround corners and between objects, but these will only be apparent if we use the photon map for direct viewing. In the next section we will see why this is not a problem for indirect viewing. Note that we store the photons before they

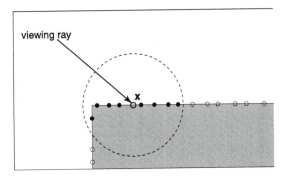

Figure 14.2. All photons (shown as black dots) within a certain radius sphere of **x** are used even if they are on a different surface than the one being used.

interact with surfaces (i.e., the incident photons). This is because we want to be able to light textured surfaces. Suppose we had a texture map with thin black and white stripes. If we stored outgoing photons we would have implicitly used the reflectance and it would be blurred as well. By storing incident photons we blur the incident lighting and keep any reflectance patterns crisp.

To use the photons we find all photons within a radius r of **x**. We assume that the surface is locally flat within this sphere. If r is chosen too small there will not be enough photons in the sphere and we will get too much noise. If r is chosen too large we will get many photons, but we will blur the features in the lighting. In practice it works well to expand r until some desired number n photons are inside the sphere. This is an "n-nearest neighbor" query.

Regardless of how many photons n we choose, the way to estimate the radiance is the same. Recall the transport equation for Section 11.7 (Figure 14.3):

$$L_s(\mathbf{k}_o) = \int_{\text{all } \mathbf{k}_i} \rho(\mathbf{k}_i, \mathbf{k}_o) L_f(\mathbf{k}_i) \cos \theta_i d\sigma_i$$

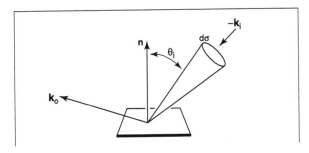

Figure 14.3. The geometry for the transport equation in its directional form.

We need to discretize this using photons to estimate L_f. Recall from the definition of radiance:

$$L_f(\mathbf{k}_i) = \frac{\Delta\Phi}{\Delta A \cos\theta_i \, \Delta\sigma}.$$

If we take the $\Delta\Phi$ to be all the power in the photons in the sphere and directional bin, we need to estimate ΔA. If we assume all the photons in the sphere hit the surface containing $\mathbf{x}$ then

$$\Delta A = \pi r^2,$$

where r is the radius of the sphere. If the n photons have powers $\Delta\Phi_1, \Delta\Phi_2, \ldots,$ $\Delta\Phi_n$, then we can plug the discretized L_f into the transport equation:

$$L_s(\mathbf{k}_o) \approx \sum_k \rho(\mathbf{k}_k, \mathbf{k}_o) \frac{\Delta\Phi_k}{\pi r^2 \cos\theta_{ik} \, \Delta\sigma_k} \cos\theta_{ik}\Delta\sigma_k$$

Note that because the $\Delta\sigma_k$ cancels, we can easily push the number of bins to infinity, so each bin has zero or one photons. This allows us to sum over the photons:

$$L_s(\mathbf{k}_o) \approx \sum_{i=1}^{n} \rho(\mathbf{k}_j, \mathbf{k}_o) \frac{\Delta\Phi_j}{\pi r^2}.$$

where $\mathbf{k}_j$ is the direction the jth photon comes from.

14.3   INDIRECT USE OF THE PHOTON MAP

In practice too many photons are needed to use photon maps for all lighting computations. However, if diffusely scattered viewing rays use the photon map, the blurring wont really be noticeable because the results of many secondary rays are averaged. In practice this means that only after the first diffuse bounce of a viewing ray should the photon map be used. This means few photons are needed.

Another way to reduce the number of photons needed is to not store direct lighting in the photon map. This means normal direct lighting computations should be done with shadow rays, and only "indirect" photons should be stored. This implies that photons should only be stored after they have scattered from a surface.

14.4   NOTES

Photon mapping has its roots in *Some Techniques for Shading Machine Renderings of Solids* (Appel, AFIPS 1968 Spring Joint Computer Conference, 1968). Such rays were used for specular effects in *Backward Ray Tracing*, (Arvo, Developments in Ray Tracing, SIGGRAPH 1986 Course Notes). Henrik Wann Jensen has developed the modern photon mapping algorithm and detailed it in his book *Realistic Image Synthesis Using Photon Mapping* (A K Peters, 2001). We've found the code in that book to work well, and we use Jensen's code for photon-searching in our own renderer.

15 | Participating Media

The previous chapters have assumed that our scene is composed of surfaces with clear air between them. This ignores the visual effects of *participating media* such as steam, dust, smoke, and water vapor. In this chapter, we discuss the transport equations for participating media, as well as path-tracing and photon-mapping strategies for rendering participating media.

15.1 TRANSPORT IN PARTICIPATING MEDIA

We assume that the medium has at each point $\mathbf{x}$ a function a that describes the probability per unit length that the light interacts with the particles in the medium, i.e., the probability that a particle interacts when traveling a distance Δs is

$$\text{probability of interaction} = a(\mathbf{x})\Delta s.$$

If the particle does interact, it is either scattered with probability $R(\mathbf{x})$ or absorbed with probability $1 - R(\mathbf{x})$. This R is often called the *single scattering albedo*. Here, the scattering albedo is analogous to directional hemispherical reflectance on surfaces, but there is no directional component because we assume the particles are randomly oriented in space and vary only in their density.

When the particles do scatter, they do so based only on the angle θ between incident and outgoing directions. This is described by the *phase function* $p(\theta)$, a probability density function defined over outgoing directions θ.

When we consider the radiance of a viewing ray parameterized by distance s, increasing toward the viewer, we have a position $\mathbf{x}(s)$. The medium properties $L(\mathbf{x}(s), \mathbf{k})$, $R(\mathbf{x}(s))$, and $a(\mathbf{x}(s))$ vary with position (and direction, in the case of radiance). To simplify the notation we will use the shorthand $L(s, \mathbf{k})$, $R(s)$, and $a(s)$ for these. The phase function varies with the angle between $\mathbf{k}$ and incident direction $\mathbf{k}_i$ and is denoted $p(s, \mathbf{k}_i)$. The ways light interacts over a short distance Δs is shown in Figure 15.1.

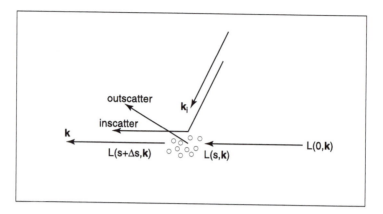

Figure 15.1. The radiance changes along a ray as light is scattered in or out or absorbed.

The radiance just after traveling through Δs changes by a small amount:

$$L(s + \Delta s, \mathbf{k}) = (1 - a(s)\Delta s)\, L(s, \mathbf{k}) + R(s)a(s)\Delta s \int_{\text{all } \mathbf{k}_i} p(s, \mathbf{k}_i)L(s, \mathbf{k}_i)d\sigma_i$$

$$(15.1)$$

Here $a(s)\Delta s$ is the fraction of light that interacts with the medium.

15.2 DIRECT LIGHTING

The direct lighting in a medium is the light that has scattered exactly once between the luminaire and the viewer, and is responsible for almost all of the appearance of "thin" media such as smoke in a room or a light fog. To compute it we note that the integral in Equation 15.1 is just an integral over the luminaire

$$L(s + \Delta s, \mathbf{k}) = (1 - a(s)\Delta s)\, L(s, \mathbf{k}) + R(s)a(s)\Delta s p(s, \mathbf{k}_i)L(s, \mathbf{k}_i)\Delta \sigma_i,$$

where $\Delta \sigma_i$ is the solid angle of the light source as seen from $\mathbf{x}(s)$. We can step back-to-front in the volume and at each s we send a ray to the light to compute $L(s, \mathbf{k}_i)$. We step along the shadow ray in steps of Δt to accumulate opacity (Figure 15.2). At each step we have

$$\alpha = (1 - a(t)\Delta t)\alpha.$$

We initialize α to be one. We can step in either direction.

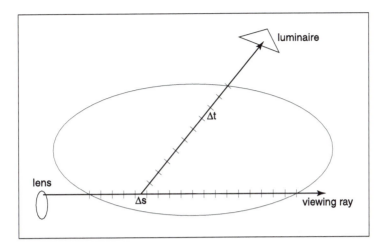

Figure 15.2. The direct lighting in a volume is generated by marching by steps of length Δs toward the eye and from each of these a shadow ray is sent and opacity is accumulated.

15.3 INDIRECT LIGHTING

To approximate indirect lighting, we can just set $L(s, \mathbf{k}_i) = C$ and then

$$\int_{\text{all } \mathbf{k}_i} p(s, \mathbf{k}) C d\sigma_i = C.$$

This is just like ambient lighting for surfaces. Alternatively we can trace photons through the volume and then use photon mapping. When a photon hits the volume we step through the volume as with viewing rays and compute probability of interaction. When an interaction takes place, we store location, direction, and power. If the interaction is not an absorbsion, we scatter the photon according to the phase function p and continue.

To use the photon map, we discretize the sum over angles:

$$R(s)a(s)\Delta s \int_{\text{all } \mathbf{k}_i} p(s, \mathbf{k}) L(s, \mathbf{k}_i) d\sigma_i \approx R(s)a(s)\Delta s \sum_j p(s, \mathbf{k}_j) L(s, \mathbf{k}_j).\Delta\sigma_j$$

Because we stores incident photons whenever they interacted with the medium (power $\Delta\Phi_j$ and direction $\mathbf{k}_j$), we can get an estimate of radiance in a given direction. If we take a disk oriented toward $\mathbf{k}$ with cross-sectional area ΔA and thickness Δb, then we would expect the power of light that interacts with the medium to be

$$\Delta\Phi^p = a\Delta b\Phi,$$

where $\Delta\Phi^p$ is the power that interacts, and $\Delta\Phi$ is the total power flowing through the volume. From definition of radiance we have:

$$L(\mathbf{k}_i) = \frac{\Delta\Phi}{\Delta A \Delta\sigma}.$$

This suggests

$$R(s)a(s)\Delta s \int_{\text{all } \mathbf{k}_i} p(s,\mathbf{k})L(s,\mathbf{k}_i)d\sigma_i \approx R(s)a(s)\Delta s \sum_j p(s,\mathbf{k}_j)\frac{\Delta\Phi_j}{\Delta A \Delta\sigma_j}\Delta\sigma_j.$$

But what we store is the power that interacts with the medium, which yields

$$R(s)a(s)\Delta s \int_{\text{all } \mathbf{k}_i} p(s,\mathbf{k})L(s,\mathbf{k}_i)d\sigma_i \approx R(s)a(s)\Delta s \sum_j p(s,\mathbf{k}_j)\frac{\Delta\Phi_j^p}{a(s)\Delta A \Delta b}.$$

Note that $\Delta A \Delta b = \Delta V$ and the as cancel:

$$R(s)a(s)\Delta s \int_{\text{all } \mathbf{k}_i} p(s,\mathbf{k})L(s,\mathbf{k}_i)d\sigma_i \approx R(s) \sum_j p(s,\mathbf{k}_j)\frac{\Delta\Phi_j^p}{\Delta V}.$$

For a sphere, $\Delta V = (4/3)\pi r^3$.

15.4 DATA FOR MEDIA

There are three pieces of data needed: a, R, and p. Typically p and R are constant for a volume and a is varied by a solid texture function such as Perlin turbulence. A comonly used p is the Henyey-Greenstein phase function:

$$p(\theta,\phi) = \frac{1-g^2}{4\pi\left(1+g^2-2g\cos\theta\right)^{1.5}}.$$

Here, g is a tuning parameter, with $g = 0$ giving isotropic scattering, and g closer to 1 being appropriate for forward-scattering media such as fog. The albedo R should be close to one for things like fog, and closer to zero for smoke.

To scatter photons in the photon-tracing stage, we use the techiques from Chapter 10 to map two Canonical random numbers (r_1, r_2) to a direction. We have $\phi = 2\pi r_1$ and the 1D density on θ:

$$q(\theta) = \frac{(1-g^2)\sin\theta}{2\left(1+g^2-2g\cos\theta\right)^{1.5}}$$

The cumulative density function is

$$Q(\theta) = \frac{1 - g^2}{2g} \left((1 - g^2 - 2g)^{-0.5} - (1 + g^2 - 2g \cos \theta)^{-0.5} \right).$$

We set $r_2 = Q(\theta)$ and then solve for $Q(\theta)$. This yields

$$\cos \theta = \frac{1}{2g} \left(1 + g^2 - \left(\frac{1 - g^2}{1 + g - 2gr_2} \right)^2 \right). \tag{15.2}$$

15.5 NOTES

A very nice review of participating media is available in Jensen's book *Realistic Image Synthesis Using Photon Mapping* (A K Peters, 2001). Equation 15.2 is not quite the same as the related equation in that book, but it does produce the same distributions, so readers should not fear there is a typographical error in either book. More information on generating the density functions for media procedurally can be found in *Texturing & Modeling: A Procedural Approach* (Ebert et. al, Morgan Kaufman, Third Edition, 2002).

16 | Going Further

This book has described how to implement a basic ray tracer and the classic probabilistic extensions. There are many places you can take it from here:

- **More shapes.** In addition to triangles and spheres, you can implement any primitive with which you can intersect a 3D line. A variety of these can be found in *An Introduction to Raytracing* (edited by Glassner, Academic Press, 1989). Perhaps the most important graphics primitive other than triangles are NURBS, whose intersection is covered in "Practical Ray Tracing of Trimmed NURBS Surfaces" (Martin et al., *Journal of Graphics Tools*, 2000).

- **Procedural models.** These include *displacement maps* that displace positions based on a procedural function, and ecosystem simulations that populate terrains with instanced plants. These are discussed in "Rendering Complex Scenes with Memory-Coherent Ray Tracing" (Pharr et al., *Proceedings of SIGGRAPH 97, Computer Graphics Proceedings, Annual Conference Series*, 1997) and "Realistic Modeling and Rendering of Plant Ecosystems" (Deussen et al., *Proceedings of SIGGRAPH 98, Computer Graphics Proceedings, Annual Conference Series*, 1998).

- **Natural illumination.** Your images will look more realistic if you use reasonable values for sunlight and skylight. These are discussed in *A Practical Analytic Model for Daylight* (Preetham et al., *Proceedings of SIGGRAPH 99, Computer Graphics Proceedings, Annual Conference Series*, 1999).

- **Subsurface scattering.** Materials such as cheese and marble get a glow from light that penetrates objects and reemerges. A method for handling this is described in "A Rapid Hierarchical Rendering Technique for Translucent Materials" (Jensen and Buhler, *Transactions on Graphics (Proc. SIGGRAPH '02)*, 2002).

- **Interactive ray tracing.** Processors are now fast enough that ray tracing can be done automatically for small image sizes on a single machine.

Two such systems are described in "Interactive Ray Tracing" (Parker et al., *Symposium on Interactive 3D Computer Graphics*, 1999) and "Interactive Distributed Ray-Tracing of Highly Complex Models" (Wald et al., *Eurographics Rendering Workshop*, 2001).

Index